A Present
Peace

A Present Peace

90 *Our Daily Bread* Reflections
for Embracing God's Truth through Hard Times

Bill Crowder

Our Daily Bread
Publishing.

A Present Peace: 90 Our Daily Bread *Reflections for Embracing God's Truth through Hard Times*
©2022 by Our Daily Bread Ministries

Interior design: Jessica Ess, Hillspring Books

Library of Congress Cataloging-in-Publication Data

Names: Crowder, Bill, author.
Title: A present peace : 90 our daily bread reflections for embracing God's truth through hard times / Bill Crowder.
Description: Grand Rapids, MI : Our Daily Bread Publishing, [2022] | Summary: "Find hope, confidence, and comfort in these 90 readings by Bill Crowder that point you to almighty God when life takes unexpected turns"-- Provided by publisher.
Identifiers: LCCN 2022025802 | ISBN 9781640701946
Subjects: LCSH: Peace of mind--Religious aspects--Christianity--Meditations. | Consolation--Meditations. | BISAC: RELIGION / Christian Living / Devotional | RELIGION / Inspirational
Classification: LCC BV4908.5 .C76 2022 | DDC 242/.4--dc23/eng/20220907
LC record available at https://lccn.loc.gov/2022025802

Printed in the United States of America
23 24 25 26 27 28 29 30 / 9 8 7 6 5 4 3 2

FOREWORD

. . .

It had been the toughest of weeks. On a Thursday in late August 2003, while on his lunchtime run, my good friend and running buddy collapsed. Before help could arrive, Kurt DeHaan ran into the presence of Jesus.

That friend had also been my gifted and highly productive boss. As the managing editor for *Our Daily Bread*, Kurt had shepherded the much-loved daily devotional for years. Along the way, he mentored this (then) young assistant editor.

Suddenly we had a void in a critical position. Who would we turn to?

One week later, my team leader invited me to a meeting with senior leadership. I expected a discussion on what to do until we hired a replacement. I was wrong. The plan was already in place. I was to receive a battlefield promotion. That meant I would be attempting to step into Kurt's dauntingly unfillable shoes.

A strange cloud of emotions hovered over me. Still stunned and grieving over my friend's permanent absence, I was scared. Intimidated. Overwhelmed. I felt wholly inadequate. Yet, at the same time, I felt strangely honored too.

My team leader that day was Bill Crowder. As we left the meeting, he looked at me. "I know just how you feel," he said, compassion saturating his voice. The tears in his eyes told me he truly did. And his smile, genuine and full of empathy, let me know we'd be okay. I still had a mentor. We were in this together. And together we would rely on our heavenly Father to show us the next steps. (I'm still waiting for Bill to run with me, though.)

For me, that moment encapsulates the heart of Bill Crowder: *we're in this together.* His concern for others infuses his communication, both written and spoken, with authenticity. Whether in casual conversations or emails, or in formal sermons or books, Bill unfailingly brings us his warmly relational style. Then he relates it to God's story and shows us how to gather strength and encouragement from it. God has given this man a pastoral heart.

Bill brings that pastor's heart to these pages. He tells stories—eminently human stories from all of life that intertwine with the grand story God is telling. That's what makes *A Present Peace* so helpful and so readable. Bill sees these stories everywhere he goes and in everything he does, reads, views, and hears.

Often, he lives these stories himself. Before Bill came to Christ, he suffered a terrible fall of over thirty feet. It should have killed him. While slowly recovering in the hospital, the family of the man he shared a room with introduced him to Jesus. The direction of Bill's life forever changed. Bill now sees God's presence in everything because he senses that presence in his own life. He knows what he's been rescued from.

Bill Crowder could be with me in that difficult moment in 2003 because he understood what God's promises had meant for him. Our heavenly Father is with us in every moment. We really are in this together.

—*Tim Gustafson*
Senior Content Editor
Our Daily Bread Ministries

Shalom

The title for this volume, *A Present Peace*, feels a little ironic to me. As I write this, I am trying desperately to meet the deadline on another book project. The subject of the book? Worry . . . in one sense, the opposite of peace. Hence, the irony.

Many of us can identify with the old standard by Jill Jackson-Miller, "Let There Be Peace on Earth." Peace seems to be an ethereal cloud, for there are so many forces in this broken world that can erode it. But I suspect that peace is also challenging because it is so frequently misunderstood. We often think of peace as the absence of conflict—as when a peace treaty is signed to bring the hostilities of war to an end. Yes, that is certainly one aspect of peace—but it is *not* the kind of peace the Bible describes and offers to us.

The biblical concept of peace is captured in the Hebrew term *shalom*. This is a very specific word that speaks of a quality of life. One writer puts it this way, "*Shalom* is more than just simply peace; it is a complete peace. It is a feeling of contentment, completeness, wholeness, well-being, and harmony."* What a difference! Peace is so much more than cessation of conflict—peace is the presence of

---

* Brenda Fawkes, "Shalom, the Peace That Passes Understanding," Regent Christian Online Academy, March 28, 2018, https://rcoa.ca/shalom-the-peace-that-passes-understanding/.

a sense of wholeness that can only come through relationship with God. This is perhaps why, in Jewish circles, *shalom* is used both to greet and to bid farewell. It is as if the speaker is wishing that kind of wholeness to the person he or she is addressing.

So, what does the Bible have to say about this kind of peace? In Psalm 4:8, the singer shares that it is this shalom peace that allows him to sleep at night, saying, "In peace I will lie down and sleep, for you alone, Lord, make me dwell in safety." Perhaps more familiarly, in the New Testament we hear Jesus offer this peace to His disciples in the upper room the night before the cross. As they are in turmoil over Jesus's announcement of His soon departure, the Master told them, "I have told you these things, so that in me you may have peace. In this world you will have trouble. But take heart! I have overcome the world" (John 16:33).

Paul connected this sense of peace to a prayer relationship with our heavenly Father when he told the church at Philippi that they could commit their needs and concerns to God in prayer. "And the peace of God," he continued, "which transcends all understanding, will guard your hearts and your minds in Christ Jesus" (Philippians 4:6–7). The Greek word for peace in the New Testament is *eirene,* which carries the idea of rest and quietness—much like shalom speaks of content-ment or wholeness.

This is what the Scriptures offer to us. I trust that as you read these devotions the Scriptures will point you to the Father who is the author of this peace. A true sense that all is well—as expressed in the classic hymn by W. D. Cornell appropriately entitled "Wonderful Peace":

> Peace, peace, wonderful peace
> Coming down from the Father above
> Sweep over my spirit forever, I pray
> In fathomless billows of love

May you know His great peace today.

—*Bill Crowder*

· REFLECTIONS ·

A Present Peace

Psalm 23

Even though I walk through the darkest valley,
I will fear no evil, for you are with me;
your rod and your staff, they comfort me. *Psalm 23:4*

When our first child was born, my wife, Marlene, was in labor for more than thirty hours, creating tremendous stress for both her and the baby. The doctor, a fill-in for her regular physician, was unfamiliar with her and her pregnancy. As a result, he waited too long to make the decision to perform an emergency Caesarean section, and the resulting trauma put our infant son in the neo-natal intensive care unit. We were told by the doctors that there was nothing they could do to help our baby to overcome his trauma-induced condition.

But by God's grace, Matt recovered. I cannot remember any moment in my life as terrifying as when I stood by his crib in intensive care. Yet I knew the Lord was near as I talked with Him through prayer.

In the terrifying moments of life (and all the other moments as well) nothing can bring comfort to the hurting heart like the reality of God's presence and care. The psalmist David wrote, "Even though I walk through the darkest valley, I will fear no evil, for you are with me; your rod and your staff, they comfort me" (Psalm 23:4).

When fear is overwhelming, the Lord is there. His comforting presence will carry us through our deepest trials.

• • •

Peace is the presence of God.

Change of Direction

> They themselves report . . . how you turned to God
> from idols to serve the living and true God. *1 Thessalonians 1:9*

The United States Secret Service was founded in 1865. Their mission? To deal with counterfeiters in an attempt to protect the dollar and, as a result, America's national economy. This targeted group of law enforcement officers, however, experienced a change of direction in 1902. They became best known for protecting the President of the United States, although their charge still embodies a variety of tasks.

Sometimes a change of direction is just what is needed. Take, for instance, the completely altered lives of the believers at Thessalonica. They had a spiritual transformation that turned their lives completely around, and it was noticed by people far and wide. Paul wrote, "You turned to God from idols to serve the living and true God" (1 Thessalonians 1:9). And "you became a model to all the believers in Macedonia and Achaia—your faith in God has become known everywhere" (vv. 7–8). The change of direction they displayed was dramatic, to say the least—abandoning the worship of idols to embrace relationship with the true and living God. And people noticed the difference in their lives.

I wonder—do people recognize the profound change Jesus has made in our hearts and lives?

• • •

Coming to Christ is not merely informational;
it's transformational.

Legal versus Right

Acts 5:17–29

*Peter and the other apostles replied: "We must obey God
rather than human beings!" Acts 5:29*

In his powerful book *Unspeakable*, Os Guinness wrestles with the problem of evil in the world. In one section, he focuses on the Nuremberg trials that followed World War II. The Nazis stood charged with crimes against humanity, and their mantra of defense was simple: "I was merely following orders." The verdict, however, was that the soldiers had a moral obligation to defy orders that, though legal, were clearly wrong.

In a much different context, Peter and the disciples were arrested for presenting the message of the risen Christ, and they were brought before the religious rulers in Jerusalem. Rather than allowing themselves to be shaped by the mood of the mob, the disciples declared their intention to continue preaching Christ.

The orders of the religious establishment may have been legal, but they were wrong. When the disciples chose to obey God rather than the godless religious leaders, they chose a standard of conviction that rose above the opinions of the rulers of this world.

The trials we face may test our commitment. But we will find opportunities to exalt the King if we trust Him for the strength to go beyond the words of the crowd-pleasers and do right as He defines it in His Word.

• • •

We must choose daily the way of the cross
over the way of the crowd. —Rick Warren

Tears in Heaven

Revelation 21:1–8

> "[God] will wipe every tear from their eyes.
> There will be no more death" or mourning or crying. *Revelation 21:4*

In 1991, famed British guitarist Eric Clapton was stricken with grief when his four-year-old son Conor died as a result of a fall from an apartment window. Looking for an outlet for his grief, Clapton penned perhaps his most poignant ballad: "Tears in Heaven." It seems that every note weighs heavy with the sense of pain and loss that can be understood only by a parent who has lost a child.

Surprisingly, however, Clapton said in a television interview years later, "In a sense, it wasn't even a sad song. It was a song of belief. When it [says that] there will be no more tears in heaven, I think it's a song of optimism—of reunion."

The thought of a heavenly reunion is powerful indeed. For everyone who has trusted Jesus Christ for salvation, there is the sure hope that we will be reunited forever in a place where God "will wipe every tear from [our] eyes. There will be no more death or mourning or crying" (Revelation 21:4). And, most of all, it is a place where we will "see [Jesus's] face" and forever be with our Savior (22:4).

In our times of loss and grief, of tears and sorrow, isn't it comforting to know that Christ has purchased for us a heavenly home where there will be no more tears!

• • •

When God wipes our tears, sorrow will give way to eternal song.

Who's the Boss?

Romans 6:1–14

Sin shall no longer be your master,
because you are not under law, but under grace. *Romans 6:14*

As my wife was babysitting our two young grandsons, they began to argue over a toy. Suddenly, the younger (by three years) forcefully ordered his older brother, "Cameron, go to your room!" Shoulders slumped under the weight of the reprimand, the dejected older brother began to slink off to his room when my wife said, "Cameron, you don't have to go to your room. Nathan's not the boss of you!" That realization changed everything, and Cam, smiling, sat back down to play.

As followers of Christ, the reality of our brokenness and our inclination to sin can assume a false authority much like that younger brother. Sin noisily threatens to dominate our hearts and minds, and the joy drains from our relationship with the Savior.

But through the death and resurrection of Christ, that threat is an empty one. Sin has no authority over us. That is why Paul wrote, "Sin shall no longer be your master, because you are not under law, but under grace" (Romans 6:14).

While our brokenness is very real, Christ's grace enables us to live in a way that pleases God and expresses His transforming power to the world. Sin is no longer our boss. We now live in the grace and presence of Jesus. His dominion in our lives releases us from the bondage of sin.

• • •

God pursues us in our restlessness, receives us in our sinfulness,
holds us in our brokenness. —Scotty Smith

Peaceful Anxiety

Philippians 4:4–13

The peace of God . . . will guard your hearts
and your minds in Christ Jesus. *Philippians 4:7*

I was scheduled to teach at a Bible conference outside the United States and was waiting for my visa to be approved. It had been rejected once, and time was slipping away. Without the visa, I would lose an opportunity for ministry, and my colleagues in that country would have to find another speaker at the last minute.

During those stressful days, a coworker asked how I felt about it all. I told him I was experiencing "peaceful anxiety." When he looked at me rather quizzically, I explained: "I have had anxiety because I need the visa and there is nothing I can do about it. But I have great peace because I know that, after all, there is nothing I can do about it!"

It's comforting to know that such things are in our Father's hands. My inability to do anything about the problem was more than matched by my confidence in God, for whom all things are possible. As I prayed about the situation, my anxiety was replaced by His peace (Philippians 4:6–7).

The problems of life can be taxing on us—physically, emotionally, and spiritually. Yet, as we learn to trust in the Father's care, we can have the peace that not only surpasses all understanding but also overcomes our anxiety. We can be at rest, for we are in God's hands.

• • •

God will keep our minds at peace.

The Right Help

Psalm 18:6–13

In my distress I called to the LORD; I cried to my God for help. . . .
My cry came before him, into his ears. *Psalm 18:6*

On a recent radio program, the hosts spoke with a "crisis management" expert about how a celebrity can recover from a public relations disaster. This specialist said one of the keys was to build strong allies who can help the star rehabilitate his or her image. In other words, it is vital when in trouble to get the right help.

That is wise counsel, for at the heart of all crisis management is recognizing that we can't accomplish everything on our own. Some challenges are too big. Some mountains are too high. In our own seasons of crisis, it is critical that we have help. That's why it's comforting to know that we have the strongest ally possible.

King David knew about that ally. In Psalm 18:6, he affirmed, "In my distress I called to the LORD; I cried to my God for help. From his temple he heard my voice; my cry came before him, into his ears." There is no greater help in our time of need than God. He alone can carry us through the trials and crises of life, and we have His word that He will never leave us nor forsake us (Hebrews 13:5).

When crisis hits, we don't have to stand alone. We have the right help. We can depend on God to be the greatest ally we could ever know. Lean on Him.

• • •

Our greatest hope here below is to get help from God above.

"Sin Makes Us Stupid"

Romans 7:14–25

*Let us throw off everything that hinders
and the sin that so easily entangles.* Hebrews 12:1

I was having lunch with a pastor-friend when the discussion sadly turned to a mutual friend in ministry who had failed morally. As we grieved together over this fallen comrade, now out of ministry, I wondered aloud, "I know anyone can be tempted and anyone can stumble, but he's a smart guy. How could he think he could get away with it?" Without blinking, my friend responded, "Sin makes us stupid." It was an abrupt statement intended to get my attention, and it worked.

I have often thought of that statement in the ensuing years, and I continue to affirm the wisdom of those words. How else can you explain the actions of King David, the man after God's own heart turned adulterer and murderer? Or the reckless choices of Samson? Or the public denials of Christ by Peter, the most public of Jesus's disciples? We are flawed people who are vulnerable to temptation and to the foolishness of mind that can rationalize and justify almost any course of action if we try hard enough.

If we are to have a measure of victory over the power of sin, it will come only as we lean on the strength and wisdom of Christ (Romans 7:24–25). As His grace strengthens our hearts and minds, we can overcome our own worst inclination to make foolish choices.

• • •

God's Spirit is your power source—
don't let sin break the connection.

Scared to Death

1 Corinthians 15:51–58

Our Savior, Christ Jesus . . . destroyed death and has brought life
and immortality to light through the gospel. *2 Timothy 1:10*

The opening line of a country song, "Sarabeth is scared to death . . . ,"
leads the listener into the fearful heart of a teenage girl who is di-
agnosed with cancer. The lyrics of "Skin (Sarabeth)" expose the
struggles she faces, not only with the disease and its treatment but
also with the obvious evidence of her struggle—the loss of her hair
(hence, the title). It is a touching song of triumph in the midst of
tragedy, as Sarabeth deals with the understandable life-and-death
fears that cancer brings.

The specter of death is faced by every human being. Yet, whether
we face that reality with fear or with confidence is not dependent on
having a good outlook or a positive attitude. The way we face death
depends completely on whether or not we have a personal relationship
with Jesus, who gave himself to die so death itself could be abolished.

Paul wrote to Timothy that our Savior was the One who "destroyed death and has brought life and immortality to light through
the gospel" (2 Timothy 1:10). The result is that even in the most
disturbing times of life, we never need to be scared to death.

• • •

We can live confidently and filled with hope,
because Jesus conquered death.

Officer Waxworks

John 14:15–24

If you love me, keep my commands. John 14:15

For several years, our family lived in Southern California while I was pastoring a church there. The community in which we lived didn't have the resources to fully patrol the streets with police. So, there was a genuine concern about the lack of safety as a result of reckless driving.

In response to the situation, city officials came up with a solution they called Officer Waxworks. Uniformed mannequins were placed in patrol cars alongside the road. Obviously, these "officers" couldn't pursue lawbreakers or write tickets, but just the appearance of "manned" patrol cars was enough to make people slow down. It was a creative way to trick people into obeying the law.

As believers in Christ, we shouldn't have to be forced or tricked into doing what's right. In fact, obedience can be drained of its significance if we obey only out of obligation or duty. Our desire should be to do what is pleasing to our Lord because we love Him. Jesus said, "Whoever has my commands and keeps them is the one who loves me" (John 14:21). We should "make it our goal to please him" (2 Corinthians 5:9).

• • •

Our desire to please God is our highest motive for obeying God.

Existing or Truly Living?

John 10:1–11

I have come that they may have life,
and have it to the full. *John 10:10*

On a family visit to Disneyland, I pondered the sign over the entrance arch that read, "The Happiest Place on Earth." The rest of the day I looked at the faces of the people and was impressed by the small number who were actually smiling during their visit to "The Happiest Place on Earth." I roamed the park with divided attention—trying to make sure my kids had a good time and wondering why so few adults seemed to be enjoying themselves.

As I think of that day, I am reminded of a line from an old song that says, "Life goes on, long after the thrill of living is gone." So it seems.

To live life to the fullest is qualitatively different from merely existing. In fact, Jesus said that part of His mission was to enable us to live life to the fullest: "I have come that they may have life, and have it to the full" (John 10:10). He came so that we could experience life to the full—not according to the standards of a fallen world, but life as it was intended to be. It is life according to the designs and desires of the Creator of life.

By coming to provide forgiveness for rebellious, broken people, Jesus has made it possible for us to live a life of joy and hope in a world of despair.

• • •

To know the Lord puts a song in your heart
and a smile on your face.

No Need to Panic

1 Peter 4:12–19

> Do not be surprised at the fiery ordeal that has
> come on you to test you, as though something
> strange thing were happening to you. *1 Peter 4:12*

On a Bible-teaching cruise in the Caribbean, I was listening to the customary first-day safety briefing. The precautions were vital in case the ship should have to be evacuated.

The instructions from the ship's personnel concluded with a simple but significant explanation. A specific combination of air-horn blasts, indicating a drill, would be distinctly different from those indicating a real emergency. The distinction was critical. A drill did not constitute a need to evacuate. If passengers were to panic during the drill, it could result in chaos.

When we don't understand the circumstances that surround us, it's easy to be shaken by life's alarms. Peter's generation experienced the same thing. His warning was simple: "Do not be surprised at the fiery ordeal that has come on you to test you" (1 Peter 4:12).

The trials and heartaches of life may sound like a call to evacuate—to run away or to respond to life in ways that are disheartening and destructive. But we would do well to listen more closely to our Lord. The trial may be nothing more than a reminder that our trust is to be in God, not in people. We can trust Him in those times when the alarms start to sound.

· · ·

Life's challenges are not designed to break us
but to bend us toward God.

How Long?

Psalm 13

How long, LORD? Will you forget me forever?
How long will you hide your face from me? *Psalm 13:1*

My friends Bob and Delores understand what it means to wait for answers—answers that never seem to come. When their son Jason and future daughter-in-law Lindsay were murdered in August 2004, a national manhunt was undertaken to find the killer and bring him to justice. After two years of prayer and pursuit, there were still no tangible answers to the painful questions the two hurting families wrestled with. There was only silence.

In such times, we are vulnerable to wrong assumptions and conclusions about life, about God, and about prayer. In Psalm 13, David wrestled with the problem of unanswered prayer. He questioned why the world was so dangerous, and he pleaded for answers from God.

It's a hard psalm that David sang, and it seems to be one of frustration. Yet, in the end, his doubts and fears turned to trust. Why? Because the circumstances of our struggles cannot diminish the character of God and His care for His children. In verse 5, David turned a corner. From his heart he prayed, "I trust in your unfailing love; my heart rejoices in your salvation."

In the pain and struggle of living without answers, we can always find comfort in our heavenly Father.

. . .

When we pray, God wraps us in His loving arms.

The Sounds of Sirens

Revelation 21:1–5

> He who was seated on the throne said,
> "I am making everything new!" *Revelation 21:5*

I was enjoying my son's high school soccer game when the relative calm and normalcy of that warm September afternoon was shattered by a sound both distinctive and alarming—the sound of sirens. The shrill whine seemed out of place at such a pleasant moment, and it demanded my attention. According to singer Don Henley, a siren usually means that "somebody's going to an emergency" or "somebody's going to jail." He's right. In either case, someone's day, perhaps including the law enforcement or rescue personnel, just took a turn for the worse.

As I lost my attention on the game and thought about the siren fading into the distance, it occurred to me that sirens are a reminder of a powerful reality: Our world is sadly broken. Whether the siren is the result of criminal activity or personal tragedy, it reminds us that something is desperately wrong and needs to be made right.

At such times, it helps to remember that God sees our world in its brokenness and has pledged that one day He will wipe away the old and make "everything new" (Revelation 21:5). That promise encourages us in the hardships of life, and it provides the whisper of His comfort—a whisper that can drown out even the sound of sirens.

• • •

God's whisper of comfort quiets the noise of our trials.

The Warmth of the Sun

Psalm 6

*I am worn out from my groaning. All night long I flood my bed
with weeping and drench my couch with tears.* Psalm 6:6

On a November day in 1963, the Beach Boys' Brian Wilson and Mike Love wrote a song quite unlike the band's typically upbeat tunes. It was a mournful song about love that's been lost. Mike said later, "As hard as that kind of loss is, the one good that comes from it is having had the experience of being in love in the first place." They titled it "The Warmth of the Sun."

Sorrow serving as a catalyst for songwriting is nothing new. Some of David's most moving psalms were penned in times of deep personal loss, including Psalm 6. Although we aren't told the events that prompted its writing, the lyrics are filled with grief, "I am worn out from my groaning. All night I flood my bed with weeping and drench my couch with tears. My eyes grow weak with sorrow" (vv. 6–7).

But that's not where the song ends. David knew pain and loss, but he also knew God's comfort. So he wrote, "The LORD has heard my cry for mercy; the LORD accepts my prayer" (v. 9).

In his grief, David not only found a song but he also found reason to trust God, whose faithfulness bridges all of life's hard seasons. In the warmth of His presence, our sorrows gain a hopeful perspective.

• • •

A song of sadness can turn our hearts
to the God whose joy for us is forever.

Sowing and Reaping

Galatians 6:7–9

> Do not be deceived: God cannot be mocked.
> A man reaps what he sows. *Galatians 6:7*

It seemed innocent enough at the time. I had just come home from high school and told my mom that I was going to a friend's house to play football. She insisted that I stay home and do my homework. Instead, I slipped out the back door and spent the next two hours making tackles and touchdowns in my friend's backyard. But on the last play, I was tackled into a swing set and knocked out my front tooth. It hurt like crazy—but not as badly as telling my parents.

That choice to disobey put me on a ten-year path of dental problems and pain that have continuing implications today. Ballplayer Roy Hobbs said in the movie *The Natural*, "Some mistakes you never stop paying for."

Centuries earlier, Paul captured the same idea in the universal law of sowing and reaping. He said, "A man reaps what he sows" (Galatians 6:7). Our choices often have a reach and impact that we could never imagine. Thus the apostle's words remind us to choose wisely.

The choices we make today produce the consequences we reap tomorrow. It's far better to avoid sin in the first place than to struggle to overcome its consequences.

Lord, we need Your wisdom to help us make good choices, and forgiveness when we make bad choices.

• • •

One good reason for doing the right thing today is tomorrow.

Grief Is Messy

1 Thessalonians 4:13–18

Brothers and sisters, we do not want you to be uninformed
about those who sleep in death, so that you do not grieve
like the rest of mankind, who have no hope. *1 Thessalonians 4:13*

The movie *We Are Marshall* tells of the November 14, 1970, plane crash that took the lives of most of the Marshall University football team, the coaching staff, and many community leaders of Huntington, West Virginia. Seventy-five lives were lost in the crash, which devastated the university and the community. Through the composite characters of Paul Griffen and Annie Cantrell, the film dramatizes the aftermath of the crash. Their stories intertwine because Griffen's son, Chris, was Annie's fiancé. When Chris died, their lives were plunged into pain that seemed unbearable. Why? Because, as Paul told Annie, "Grief is messy."

He was right, grief is messy. All of us grieve at one time or another—including those of us who are Christ-followers. For the believer, however, there is something beyond the tears, pain, and loss. There is hope.

Writing to a church family who had seen loved ones taken in death, Paul acknowledged the reality of grief. But he challenged them not to "grieve like the rest of mankind, who have no hope" (1 Thessalonians 4:13). Loss and death are part of life, but believers can face them, knowing that Christians never say goodbye for the last time. We can comfort one another (v. 18) with the hope of the resurrection and a future reunion.

• • •

Because Christ lives, death is not tragedy but triumph.

Wipe Away Tears

Revelation 21:1–7

> "[God] will wipe every tear from their eyes." . . .
> There will be no more . . . pain, for the old order
> of things has passed away. *Revelation 21:4*

I had just finished preaching on the heartaches of life when a couple approached me at the front of the church. The woman told me about the burden they bore as a family. Their young son had severe physical problems, and the strain of the constant care of this needy little guy, coupled with the heartache of knowing they couldn't improve his situation, sometimes felt unbearable.

As the couple shared, with tears in their eyes, their little daughter stood with them—listening and watching. Seeing the obvious hurt etched by tears on her mother's face, the girl reached up and gently wiped the tears from her mother's cheek. It was a simple gesture of love and compassion, and a profound display of concern from one so young.

Our tears often blur our sight and prevent us from seeing clearly. In those moments, it can be an encouragement to have a friend who cares enough to love us in our pain and walk with us in our struggles.

Even though friends can be a help, only Christ can reach beyond our tears and touch the deep hurts of our hearts. His comfort can carry us through the struggles of our lives until that day when God himself wipes away every tear from our eyes (Revelation 21:4).

• • •

The God who washed away our sins will also wipe away our tears.

Cracked Lenses

Psalm 141

But my eyes are fixed on you, Sovereign LORD;
in you I take refuge—do not give me over to death. *Psalm 141:8*

I started wearing glasses when I was ten years old. They are still a necessity because my sixty-something eyes are losing their battle against time. When I was younger, I thought glasses were a nuisance—especially when playing sports. Once, the lenses of my glasses got cracked while I was playing softball. It took several weeks to get them replaced. In the meantime, I saw everything in a skewed and distorted way.

In life, pain often functions like cracked lenses. It creates within us a conflict between what we experience and what we believe. Pain can give us a badly distorted perspective on life—and on God. In those times, we need our God to provide us with new lenses to help us see clearly again. That clarity of sight usually begins when we turn our eyes upon the Lord. The psalmist encouraged us to do this: "But my eyes are fixed on you, Sovereign LORD; in you I take refuge—do not give me over to death" (141:8). Seeing God clearly can help us see life's experiences more clearly.

As we turn our eyes to the Lord in times of pain and struggle, we will experience His comfort and hope in our daily lives. He will help us to see everything clearly again.

• • •

Focusing on Christ puts everything in perspective.

Hope in God

Psalm 42

Why, my soul, are you downcast? . . . Put your hope in God,
for I will yet praise him, my Savior and my God. *Psalm 42:5*

Looking at the peaceful western shores of Sri Lanka, I found it hard to imagine that a tsunami had struck just a few months earlier. The sea was calm and beautiful, couples were walking in the bright sunshine, and residents were going about their business—all giving the scene an ordinary feeling I wasn't prepared for. The impact of the disaster was still there, but it had gone underground into the hearts and minds of the survivors—the trauma and its tragic aftermath would not be easily forgotten.

It was catastrophic grief that prompted the psalmist to cry out in anguish: "My tears have been my food day and night, while people say to me all day long, 'Where is your God?'" (Psalm 42:3). The struggle of his heart had likewise been turned inward. While the rest of the world went on with business as usual, he carried in his heart the need for deep and complete healing.

Only as we submit our brokenness to the good and great Shepherd of our hearts can we find the peace that allows us to respond to life: "Why, my soul, are you downcast? Why so disturbed within me? Put your hope in God, for I will yet praise him, my Savior and my God" (v. 5).

"Put your hope in God." It's the only solution for the deep traumas of the heart.

•   •   •

No one is hopeless whose hope is in God.

The Search for Justice

Ecclesiastes 3:14–22

I saw something else under the sun:
In the place of judgment—wickedness was there,
in the place of justice—wickedness was there. *Ecclesiastes 3:16*

A trial has just ended, and the reactions to the verdict could not be more different. The family of the alleged murderer celebrates the declaration of a mistrial due to a legal technicality. Meanwhile, the grieving parents whose daughter has died wonder about a justice system that would allow such a decision. As they stand weeping before a mass of microphones and cameras, they exclaim: "Where is the justice in this? Where is the justice?"

We've seen this scenario played out in the news or on TV crime dramas. We instinctively long for justice but cannot seem to find it. The wisest man of his day, Solomon, faced a similar frustration and disappointment. He saw that imperfect human beings could never administer perfect justice. He wrote: "I saw . . . under the sun: In the place of judgment—wickedness was there, in the place of justice—wickedness was there" (Ecclesiastes 3:16).

If all we trusted in were imperfect people, we would lose all hope. But Solomon wisely added in verse 17: "God will bring into judgment both the righteous and the wicked, for there will be a time for every activity, a time to judge every deed."

The search for justice can be satisfied only by trusting the God who is always just.

• • •

Someday the scales of justice will be perfectly balanced.

Bowling a Googly

1 Peter 4:12–19

Do not be surprised at the fiery ordeal that has come on you
to test you. . . . But rejoice inasmuch as you participate
in the sufferings of Christ. *1 Peter 4:12–13*

George Bernard Shaw once said, "England and America are two countries separated by a common language." An example from the world of sports demonstrates his point.

As a lifelong baseball fan, I'm familiar with the term curveball. It's a ball thrown by the pitcher in such a way that it changes direction, fooling the opponent. In cricket, the strategy is similar but the word is very different. The bowler (pitcher) tries to overcome the batsman by "bowling a googly" (pitching a curveball).

Though games and cultures differ, the concept of the curveball portrays a reality familiar in any language. Life is full of times when we are unsuspectingly "bowled a googly," and we find ourselves overwhelmed. In those moments of fear and confusion, it's comforting to know we have a God who is sufficient for any challenge.

Trials are to be expected (1 Peter 4:12). Yet we may well be shocked by the circumstances facing us. But God is never surprised! He permits our trials, and He can enable us to respond to them in a way that honors Him.

When we suffer, we must "commit [ourselves] to [our] faithful Creator and continue to do good," wrote Peter (v. 19). In God's strength, we can face life's most troublesome curveballs.

• • •

Nothing surprises God.

No Griping

Philippians 2:12–18

Do everything without grumbling or arguing. Philippians 2:14

During my first week of Bible college, we had several days of orientation in which we were given a rule book to study. Several days later, during a meeting to discuss those rules, one student stood up and asked, "What is 'no gripping'? And why is it against the rules?"

He was referring to a statement in the rule book he had misread. Instead of "gripping," it read "griping"—complaining or grumbling.

A rule against griping is perfectly understandable. The cancer of a complaining spirit can undermine the spiritual and emotional health of an individual and can infect an entire group. This can result in discontent, frustration, and even rebellion.

Moses heard griping among God's people a mere three days after leading them from slavery into freedom (Exodus 15:24). Centuries later, Samuel felt the weight of griping as he sought to represent God to his generation (1 Samuel 8:4–9).

A complaining spirit can destroy the effectiveness of a church too. Paul wrote to the church at Philippi, "Do everything without grumbling or arguing" (Philippians 2:14).

We need to avoid a complaining spirit when serving Christ. Instead, rejoice and thank God for all He has done! No griping allowed.

• • •

When you feel like griping, start counting your blessings.

Comfort Food

Romans 15:1–7

*For everything that was written in the past
was written to teach us, so that through the endurance
taught in the Scriptures . . . we might have hope.* Romans 15:4

I love the phrase "comfort food." It speaks of the things that are so good, so familiar, so right, that they can always bring a smile to your face. For me, comfort food usually includes some form of beef and potatoes. Hamburgers and french fries. Meatloaf and mashed potatoes and gravy. Also, chocolate in almost any form imaginable. These are the foods that speak to me and say that all is well with the world. (I'm not saying they're the most healthy!)

Unfortunately, all is not well with the world, and no amount of hamburgers and french fries can make it right. Real comfort is not the byproduct of specific foods any more than it is the result of alcohol or drugs or money or pleasure or power. It is a much deeper need that requires a much deeper solution.

Paul told the church at Rome that the search for comfort can begin in the pages of the Bible. He wrote, "For everything that was written in the past was written to teach us, so that through the endurance taught in the Scriptures . . . we might have hope" (Romans 15:4).

God has given us His Word to draw us to himself. Through a relationship with Him, He provides the comfort we need to live in a broken world.

· · ·

God's Word is a life preserver that keeps the soul
from sinking in a sea of trouble.

Shark Tonic

Let us throw off everything that hinders and the sin
that so easily entangles. And let us run with perseverance
the race marked out for us. Hebrews 12:1

Have you ever heard of shark "tonic"? It isn't a serum that prevents shark attacks or a medicine given to sharks. The actual term is "tonic immobility," described as "a natural state of paralysis that animals enter. . . . Sharks can be placed in a tonic immobility state by turning them upside down. The shark remains in this state of paralysis for an average of fifteen minutes before it recovers."

Imagine, a dangerous shark can be made vulnerable simply by turning it upside down. The state of tonic immobility makes the shark incapable of movement.

Sin is like that. Our ability to honor our Lord, which we are created in Christ to do, can be put into "tonic immobility" by the power and consequences of sin. To that end, the writer of Hebrews wants us to be proactive. He wrote, "Therefore, since we are surrounded by such a great cloud of witnesses, let us throw off everything that hinders and the sin that so easily entangles. And let us run with perseverance the race marked out for us" (Hebrews 12:1).

If we are to run the race of the Christian life effectively, we must deal with sin before it immobilizes us. We need to lay aside the sin that hinders us from pleasing Him—starting today.

· · ·

We must face up to our sins before we can put them behind us.

The Innocent Man

Genesis 18:22–33

Will not the Judge of all the earth do right? *Genesis 18:25*

John Grisham is well-known for his courtroom novels—fast-paced tales of lawyers and victims, authorities and wrongdoers. However, his book *The Innocent Man* is not fiction. It is a real-life story of injustice. It tells of the brutal murder of a young woman and the two men who, though innocent, were convicted and sentenced to death for the crime. Only with the advent of DNA testing were they proven innocent and spared from execution after seventeen years of suffering wrongly. At long last, justice prevailed.

Everyone desires justice. But we must recognize that our human frailty makes it challenging to mete out true justice. And we can be bent toward revenge, making a casualty out of the pursuit of it.

It's helpful to remember that perfect justice can be found only in God. Abraham described Him with the rhetorical question, "Will not the Judge of all the earth do right?" (Genesis 18:25). The necessary answer is yes. But even more, His courtroom is the one and only place where we can be certain that justice will prevail.

In a world filled with injustice, we can take the wrongs done to us, submit them to the Judge of all the earth, and trust Him for ultimate justice.

• • •

Life is not always fair, but God is always faithful.

Flying Machines

Psalm 6

I am worn out from my groaning. All night long I flood my bed
with weeping and drench my couch with tears. *Psalm 6:6*

Recording artist James Taylor exploded onto the music scene in early 1970 with the song "Fire and Rain." In it, he talked about the disappointments of life, describing them as "sweet dreams and flying machines in pieces on the ground." That was a reference to Taylor's original band Flying Machine, whose attempt at breaking into the recording industry had failed badly, causing him to wonder if his dreams of a musical career would ever come true. The reality of crushed expectations had taken their toll, leaving Taylor with a sense of loss and hopelessness.

The psalmist David also experienced hopeless despair as he struggled with his own failures, the attacks of others, and the disappointments of life. In Psalm 6:6 he said, "I am worn out from my groaning. All night long I flood my bed with weeping and drench my couch with tears." The depth of his sorrow and loss drove him to heartache—but in that grief he turned to the God of all comfort. David's own crushed and broken "flying machines" gave way to the assurance of God's care, prompting him to say, "The Lord has heard my cry for mercy; the Lord accepts my prayer" (v. 9).

In our own seasons of disappointment, we too can find comfort in God, who cares for our broken hearts.

• • •

God's whisper of comfort quiets the noise of our trials.

What's Next?

Philippians 3:7–16

I press on toward the goal to win the prize for which God has called me heavenward in Christ Jesus. Philippians 3:14

In the television series *The West Wing*, fictional president Josiah Bartlet regularly ended staff meetings with two words: "What's next?" It was his way of signaling that he was finished with the issue at hand and ready to move on to other concerns. The pressures and responsibilities of life in the White House demanded that he not focus on what was in the rearview mirror—he needed to keep his eyes ahead, moving forward to what was next.

In a sense, the apostle Paul had a similar perspective on life. He knew that he had not "arrived" spiritually, and that he had a long way to go in becoming like Christ. What could he do? He could either fixate on the past, with its failures, disappointments, struggles, and disputes or he could learn from those things and move on to "what's next."

In Philippians 3, Paul tells us how he chose to live his life: "Forgetting what is behind and straining toward what is ahead, I press on toward the goal to win the prize for which God has called me heavenward in Christ Jesus" (vv. 13–14). It's a perspective that speaks of moving on—of embracing what's next. It is where we too must focus as we seek to be shaped into the image of the Savior while we look forward to eternity with Him.

• • •

Keep your eyes fixed on the prize.

Slapton Sands

1 Peter 5:1–11

> Be alert and of sober mind. Your enemy the devil prowls around
> like a roaring lion looking for someone to devour. *1 Peter 5:8*

On the southern shores of England is Slapton Sands. This beautiful beach area carries a tragic memory from its past.

On April 28, 1944, during World War II, Allied soldiers were engaged in Operation Tiger, a training exercise in amphibious beach landings in preparation for the D-Day invasion of Normandy. Suddenly, enemy gunboats appeared and killed over 700 American servicemen in a surprise attack. Today, a monument stands on Slapton Sands to commemorate the sacrifice of those young men who died while training for battle but were never able to enter the conflict.

This tragedy is a metaphor that warns the believer in Christ. We too are involved in combat with an enemy who is powerful and deceptive. That is why the apostle Peter warned: "Be alert and of sober mind. Your enemy the devil prowls around like a roaring lion looking for someone to devour" (1 Peter 5:8).

Like the soldiers on Slapton Sands, we face an enemy who desires our undoing. In the service of our King, we must be on the alert. The call to be effective in battle (2 Timothy 2:3–4) challenges us to be ready for the surprise attacks of our spiritual enemy—so we can endure to serve another day.

• • •

Satan's ploys are no match for the Savior's power.

The Circle of Fear

1 John 2:1–11

*If anybody does sin, we have an advocate
with the Father—Jesus Christ, the Righteous One.* 1 John 2:1

When the popular band The Eagles prepares a new song for concert, they sit in a circle with acoustic guitars and unamplified voices and rehearse their intricate vocals. They call this exercise "The Circle of Fear" because there is no place to hide and no way to conceal any errors they might make in the harmonies. That sense of absolute exposure for their mistakes is what makes this drill so frightening to them.

Apart from Christ, we would suffer a far worse kind of exposure before the God of all justice. If we had no advocate and no escape, we would also have no hope. But in Christ, the believer has a Defender who stands before the Father on our behalf. First John 2:1 says, "My dear children, I write this to you so that you will not sin. But if anybody does sin, we have an advocate with the Father—Jesus Christ, the Righteous One." With our failings exposed, He takes our defense. Our Defender carries our relationship with God beyond a "circle of fear" to a fellowship of grace and truth.

Our challenge is to live lives of purity and integrity that honor our heavenly Father. Yet, when we do fail, we do not need to fear abandonment or ridicule from our Father. We have an Advocate who will carry us through.

· · ·

The One who died as our Substitute now lives as our Advocate.

Walk the Walk

1 Timothy 4:6–16

Set an example for the believers in speech,
in conduct, in love, in faith and in purity. *1 Timothy 4:12*

The preacher was speaking tongue-in-cheek when he complained, "My wife is absolutely unreasonable. She actually expects me to live everything I preach!" It's so much easier to tell someone what is right than to practice it personally.

When my son and I play golf together, I can tell him exactly how to play the hole and hit the shots. But my own ability to hit those shots is sadly limited. I suppose this is what is meant when we refer to athletes who "talk the talk, but don't walk the walk." Anyone can talk a good game, but actually performing well is far more difficult.

This is particularly true in the challenge of following Jesus Christ. It is not enough for us to talk about faith; we must live out our faith. Perhaps that is why Paul, after giving instructions to his young protégé Timothy about how to preach, included this reminder: "Don't let anyone look down on you because you are young, but set an example for the believers in speech, in conduct, in love, in faith and in purity. . . . Be diligent in these matters; give yourself wholly to them" (1 Timothy 4:12, 15).

As Christ's followers, we do not have the luxury of just talking a good game—we must live lives of exemplary faith in Jesus Christ. We must walk the walk.

• • •

We please God when our walk matches our talk.

Beware the Rupert

2 Corinthians 11:3–4, 12–15

Satan himself masquerades as an angel of light. *2 Corinthians 11:14*

In the June 6, 1944, D-Day invasion of Europe, an armada of Allied ships assaulted the beaches of Normandy, France. Simultaneously, thousands of airplanes dropped paratroopers into the action. Along with the paratroopers, the Allies also dropped hundreds of rubber dummies behind the enemy lines. Called "Ruperts," these dummies were intended to simulate an attack to confuse the enemy. As the Ruperts landed, some German outposts were tricked into fighting the "paradummies," creating a vital crack in the walls of Fortress Europe.

We accept that kind of deception as part of a legitimate military operation designed to thwart oppressive forces. What we should not accept is the deception Satan throws our way. Paul explained that the devil "masquerades as an angel of light" (2 Corinthians 11:14), and his servants appear to be people who are promoting righteousness (v. 15).

We must be alert! Our spiritual enemy would love to have followers of Christ distracted by false teaching and faulty doctrine. But as we keep our eyes on Jesus and the clear teachings of Scripture, our Lord can keep us aimed in the right direction.

Don't be tricked by Satan's Ruperts.

• • •

God's truth uncovers Satan's lies.

Lament for a Friend

2 Samuel 1:11, 17–27

I grieve for you, Jonathan my brother;
you were very dear to me. *2 Samuel 1:26*

As a pastor, I was often asked to lead funeral services. Typically, the funeral director would give me a 3 x 5 index card with all the particulars about the deceased so I would be informed about him or her. I never got used to that, however. As practical and necessary as it may have been, it seemed a bit trite to take a person's earthly sojourn and reduce it to an index card. Life is too big for that.

After David received news of Jonathan's death, he spent time recalling the life of his friend—even writing a lament that others could sing as a way to respect Jonathan (2 Samuel 1:17–27). David recalled his friend's courage and skill, and he spoke of the grief that caused him to lament deeply. He honored a rich, pleasant, heroic life. For David, it was an intense time of mourning and remembrance.

When we grieve for a loved one, it is vital to recall the cherished details and shared experiences of our lives together. Those memories flood our hearts with far more thoughts than an index card can hold. The day that grief visits our hearts is not a time for short summaries and quick snapshots of our loved one's life. It is a time to remember deeply, giving God thanks for the details, the stories, and the impact of an entire life. It's time to pause, reflect, and honor.

• • •

Precious memories of life can temper
the profound sadness of death.

Preventing Regret

2 Samuel 18:31–19:4

*The king was shaken. He went up to the room
over the gateway and wept.* 2 Samuel 18:33

In the 1980s, the British band Mike and the Mechanics recorded a powerful song titled, "The Living Years." The songwriter mourns his father's death, because their relationship had been strained and marked by silence rather than sharing. The singer remorsefully says, "I didn't get to tell him all the things I had to say." Struggling with regret over words unsaid and love unexpressed, he laments, "I just wish I could have told him in the living years."

King David similarly regretted his broken relationship with his son Absalom. Angered over David's refusal to punish Amnon for raping his sister Tamar, Absalom killed Amnon and fled (2 Samuel 13:21–34). David's servant Joab knew that he longed to go to his fugitive son, so he arranged for Absalom to be brought to him. But their relationship was never the same again. Absalom's bitterness sparked a conflict that ended with his death (18:14). It was a bitter victory for King David, causing him to lament his lost son and their failed relationship (18:33). No amount of grieving, however, could undo David's heartache.

We can learn from David's regret when dealing with broken relationships. The pain of trying to make things right can be hard. But it's much better to do what we can to make things right "in the living years."

• • •

A broken relationship can be repaired—
but only if you're willing to try.

Power to Persevere

James 5:1–11

You have heard of Job's perseverance and have seen
what the Lord finally brought about. The Lord is full
of compassion and mercy. *James 5:11*

Professional golfer Paula Creamer had worked all year long to earn a berth in the 2008 ADT Championship, the year's final tournament on the LPGA tour. When the event began, however, Creamer was suffering from peritonitis, a painful inflammation of the abdominal wall. Throughout the four days of the tournament, she was in constant pain and unable to eat. She even spent a night in the hospital because of the condition. Still, she persevered to the end and, amazingly, she finished third. Her determination earned her many new fans.

The challenges and crises of life can tax us to the very end of our strength, and in such times it is easy to want to give up. But James offers followers of Christ another perspective. He says that while life is a battle, it is also a blessing: "We count as blessed those who have persevered. You have heard of Job's perseverance and have seen what the Lord finally brought about. The Lord is full of compassion and mercy" (James 5:11).

In Job's example, we find encouragement and the power to persevere in life's darkest hours—power rooted in God, who is compassionate and merciful. Even when life is painful and hard, we can persevere because God is there. His mercy endures forever (Psalm 136).

• • •

God provides the power we need to persevere.

The Right Information

1 Thessalonians 4:13–18

Brothers and sisters, we do not want you to be uninformed about those who sleep in death, so that you do not grieve like the rest of mankind, who have no hope. 1 Thessalonians 4:13

Our flight had been airborne about fifteen minutes when the pilot announced that the aircraft had a serious problem the crew was trying to analyze. A few minutes later, he announced that it was a vibration and that we would have to return to the airport. Then the flight attendants made a series of step-by-step announcements explaining what was going on and what would happen once we were on the ground. In an event that could have been terrifying, the fears of the passengers were relieved because we were given the right information.

In the first century, a group of believers in Thessalonica were afraid that their believing loved ones who had died were gone forever and would miss out on the second coming of Christ. For that reason, Paul wrote, "Brothers and sisters, we do not want you to be uninformed about those who sleep in death, so that you do not grieve like the rest of mankind, who have no hope" (1 Thessalonians 4:13). Paul's words of comfort were intended to soften their fears by giving them the right information, which made all the difference in the world. While grieving their loss, they could still have hope of a coming reunion with those who were in Christ.

In seasons of loss, we too can find comfort and hope because the Bible has given us the right information.

• • •

Death is not a period—it's only a comma.

He Never Sleeps

Psalm 121

He will not let your foot slip—he who watches over you
will not slumber. *Psalm 121:3*

Giraffes have the shortest sleep cycle of any mammal. They sleep only between ten minutes and two hours in a twenty-four-hour period and average just less than two hours of sleep per day. Seemingly always awake, the giraffe has nothing much in common with most humans in that regard. If we had so little sleep, it would probably mean we had some form of insomnia. But for giraffes, it's not a sleep disorder that keeps them awake. It's just the way God has made them.

If you think two hours a day is not much sleep, consider this fact about the Creator of our tall animal friends: Our heavenly Father never sleeps.

Describing God's continual concern for us, the psalmist declares, "He who watches over you will not slumber" (Psalm 121:3). In the context of this psalm, the writer makes it clear that God's sleepless vigilance is for our good. Verse five says, "The LORD watches over you." God keeps us, protects us, and cares for us—with no need for refreshing. Our Protector is constantly seeking our good.

Are you facing difficulties? Turn to the One who never sleeps. Each second of each day, let Him "watch over your coming and going" (v. 8).

•   •   •

The One who upholds the universe will never let you down.

Plausible Deniability

Psalm 51:1–10

The LORD does not look at the things people look at.
People look at the outward appearance,
but the LORD looks at the heart. *1 Samuel 16:7*

Answering media charges of scandal and impropriety, the guilty politician responded with the plea, "I have no recollection of those events." It was yet another attempt of a public figure to apply a strategy called "plausible deniability." This is when individuals try to create a personal safety net for themselves by seeking to convince others that they had no knowledge of the events in question. Someone else gets blamed and becomes the scapegoat for the guilty person's wrongs.

Sometimes Christians have their own kind of plausible deniability. We claim ignorance of our wrong behavior, rationalize, or blame others—but God knows the truth. The Bible tells us: "People look at the outward appearance, but the LORD looks at the heart" (1 Samuel 16:7). This is true whether the heart is pure or if it's a corrupt heart robed in false claims of innocence. We may fool others who see us only on the outside, but God sees the reality of our hearts—whether good or bad.

It is wise, therefore, to humbly confess our faults to the Lord. He desires that we admit the truth (Psalm 51:6). The only way to escape the sin and restore our fellowship with God is to acknowledge and confess it to Him (vv. 3–4).

• • •

We may successfully fool others, but God knows our hearts.

He Already Knows

Do not be like them, for your Father
knows what you need before you ask him. *Matthew 6:8*

A friend who is a commercial pilot told me about a flight in which he encountered a serious mechanical issue—a problem with dangerous implications. When the situation occurred, the warning lights in the cockpit informed him of the problem, and he monitored it all the way to the destination, ultimately landing safely.

Once on the ground, the pilot immediately went to the maintenance staff and reported it. To his surprise, the mechanics responded, "We already know about the problem and are ready to fix it. When you got the cockpit warning, we automatically got an electronic warning as well."

As he shared that incident, I couldn't help but compare it to Jesus's words about our heavenly Father: "Your Father knows what you need before you ask him" (Matthew 6:8). He said this in contrast to people who believe that they must "keep on babbling . . . for they think they will be heard because of their many words" (v. 7). Jesus presupposes God's knowledge of and concern for His children.

Even though God knows our needs, He still wants us to share our hearts with Him. He stands ready to hear our prayer and to repair our brokenness by His grace.

• • •

Prayer is the voice of faith, trusting that God knows and cares.

Assembly Required

Philippians 4:4–13

Do not be anxious about anything, but . . .
present your requests to God. *Philippians 4:6*

When our daughter and her fiancé began receiving wedding presents, it was a happy time. One gift they received was a bench cabinet that had to be assembled—and I volunteered for the task because they already had so much to do to prepare for the wedding. Although it took a couple of hours, it was much easier than expected. All of the wooden pieces were precut and predrilled, and all the hardware for assembly was included. The instructions were virtually foolproof.

Unfortunately, most of life isn't that way. Life doesn't carry with it simple instructions, nor do we find all of the necessary parts in hand. We face situations with no clear idea of what we're getting into or what it will take to pull it off. We can easily find ourselves overwhelmed with these difficult moments.

But we need not face our burdens alone. God wants us to bring them to Him: "Do not be anxious about anything, but . . . present your requests to God. And the peace of God . . . will guard your hearts and your minds in Christ Jesus" (Philippians 4:6–7).

We have a Savior who understands and offers His peace in the midst of our struggles.

• • •

The secret of peace is to give every anxious care to God.

No Laughing Matter

Philippians 1:12–20

Everyone who wants to live a godly life in Christ Jesus will be persecuted. 2 Timothy 3:12

As my wife and I were walking through a shopping mall, we came to a T-shirt stand. While browsing the shirts and their often humorous sayings, I noticed one with a disturbing message. It read, "So Many Christians, So Few Lions." That shirt, with its reference to the first-century practice of throwing Christians to the lions in the Colosseum in Rome, wasn't at all funny.

Persecution is no laughing matter. Not long before those brave Christians faced death in Rome's cruel sport, Paul wrote, "Everyone who wants to live a godly life in Christ Jesus will be persecuted" (2 Timothy 3:12). Persecution is inevitable, and it should be a matter of serious concern for all believers. In fact, at this very moment fellow brothers and sisters in Christ around the world are suffering in Jesus's name.

What can we do about it? First, we can pray that God will comfort them in their suffering. Second, we can aid families left without support when loved ones are imprisoned. Third, we can pray now for courage should we face persecution. When the apostle Paul was put in jail for his faith, his courage led others to be bolder in their witness (Philippians 1:14).

Want to encourage the persecuted church? Pray. Then proclaim the message for which believers suffer.

• • •

We find courage to stand when we kneel before the Lord.

The Core of the Problem

Romans 3:10–18

For I know that good itself does not dwell in me,
that is, in my sinful nature. For I have the desire
to do what is good, but I cannot carry it out. *Romans 7:18*

One of my favorite television cartoons as a boy was *Tom Terrific*. When Tom faced a challenge, he would put on his thinking cap and work through the matter with his faithful sidekick Mighty Manfred, the Wonder Dog. Usually, those problems found their source in Tom's arch-enemy, Crabby Appleton. To this day, I remember how this villain was described on the show. He was "Crabby Appleton—rotten to the core."

The fact is that all of us share Crabby Appleton's primary problem—apart from Christ, we're all rotten to the core. The apostle Paul described us this way: "There is no one righteous, not even one; there is no one who understands; there is no one who seeks God" (Romans 3:10–11). None of us are capable of living up to God's perfect standard of holiness. Because of our condition of being separated from a holy God, He sent His Son Jesus to give himself to die on the cross for the punishment we deserve, and then rise again. Now we can be "justified freely by his grace" through faith in Him (v. 24).

Jesus Christ has come to people "rotten to the core," and He makes us a "new creation" by faith in Him (2 Corinthians 5:17). In His goodness, He has fixed our problem completely—all the way down to our core.

• • •

We need more than a new start—we need a new heart.

Suit Up

Ephesians 6:13–21

Put on the full armor of God, so that when
the day of evil comes, you may be able to stand your ground,
and after you have done everything, to stand. *Ephesians 6:13*

When I played football as a kid, one thing that took some getting used to was all the equipment we had to wear. Running effectively in a helmet, shoulder pads, and a variety of other protective items can feel awkward and clumsy at first. But over time the protective gear becomes like a familiar friend that provides welcome protection against serious injury. When a football player suits up, he knows that his equipment is designed to protect him in battle against a dangerous opponent.

As followers of Christ, we also face a dangerous foe—a spiritual enemy who seeks our downfall and destruction. Fortunately, our Lord has provided us with protection, and He challenges us to suit up for spiritual battle.

In Ephesians 6:13, we read, "Put on the full armor of God, so that when the day of evil comes, you may be able to stand your ground, and after you have done everything, to stand." Paul then describes our armor—helmet, breastplate, shield, sword, belt, and shoes. These pieces of spiritual equipment are effective only if we put them on and use them—even if they might feel uncomfortable at first. Faithfulness in the Word (v. 17), in prayer (v. 18), and in witness (vv. 19–20) are critical to making our armor feel like a part of us. So suit up! The battle is on!

• • •

God's armor is tailor-made for you, but you must put it on.

Whispering Gallery

Proverbs 10:13–23

Sin is not ended by multiplying words,
but the prudent hold their tongues. *Proverbs 10:19*

London's domed St. Paul's Cathedral has an interesting architectural phenomenon called the "whispering gallery." One website explains it this way: "The name comes from the fact that a person who whispers facing the wall on one side can be clearly heard on the other, since the sound is carried perfectly around the vast curve of the Dome."

In other words, you and a friend could sit on opposite sides of architect Sir Christopher Wren's great cathedral and carry on a conversation without having to speak above a whisper.

While that may be a fascinating feature of St. Paul's Cathedral, it can also be a warning to us. What we say about others in secret can travel just as easily as whispers travel around that gallery. And not only can our gossip travel far and wide but often it can also do great harm along the way.

Perhaps this is why the Bible frequently challenges us about the ways we use words. The wise King Solomon wrote, "Sin is not ended by multiplying words, but the prudent hold their tongues." (Proverbs 10:19).

Instead of using whispers and gossip that can cause hurt and pain while serving no good purpose, we would do better to restrain ourselves and practice silence.

• • •

Gossip ends at a wise person's ears.

Never Alone

Hebrews 13:1–8

> Keep your lives free from the love of money
> and be content with what you have, because God has said,
> "Never will I leave you; never will I forsake you." *Hebrews 13:5*

Having played intercollegiate soccer, I've never lost my love for "The Beautiful Game." I especially enjoy watching the English Premier League. One reason is the skill and speed with which the game is played there. Also, I love the way the fans sing in support of their beloved "sides." For instance, Liverpool has for years had "You'll Never Walk Alone" as its theme. How moving to hear 50,000 fans rise as one to sing the lyrics of that old standard! It's an encouragement to players and fans alike that together they will see each other through to the end. Walk alone? Never.

This sentiment has meaning for everyone. Because each of us is made for community, isolation and loneliness are among the most painful of human experiences. During painful times, our faith is vital.

The child of God never needs to fear abandonment. Even if people turn on us, friends forsake us, or circumstances separate us from loved ones, we are never alone. God has said, "Never will I leave you; never will I forsake you" (Hebrews 13:5). This is not just a nice tune or clever lyrics offering an empty sentiment. It is the promise of God himself to those who are the objects of His love. He is there—and He isn't going away.

With Christ, you will never walk alone.

• • •

God's presence with us is one of His greatest presents to us.

Bull Sharks

1 Peter 4:12–19

Dear friends, do not be surprised at the fiery ordeal
that has come on you to test you. 1 Peter 4:12

Following a recent lunch discussion, I decided to research the comment that a bull shark attack had once occurred in Lake Michigan. It seemed like such an impossible thought that we all scoffed at the idea of sharks in a freshwater lake so far away from any ocean. I found one online site that claimed a bull shark attack did occur in Lake Michigan in 1955, but it was never verified. A shark attack in Lake Michigan? If the story were true, it would definitely be a rare occurrence.

Wouldn't it be great if hard times were like Lake Michigan bull shark attacks—rare or even untrue? But they aren't. Hardships and difficulties are common. It's just that when they happen to us, we think they shouldn't.

Perhaps that is why the apostle Peter, writing to first-century followers of Christ going through tough times, said, "Dear friends, do not be surprised at the fiery ordeal that has come to test you, as though something strange were happening to you" (1 Peter 4:12). These trials are not abnormal—and once we get past our surprise, we can turn to the Father who ministers deeply to our hearts and in our lives. He has a love that never fails. And in our world filled with trials, that kind of love is desperately needed.

• • •

By the sunshine of His love,
God paints on our clouds the rainbow of His grace.

A Hard Goodbye

Psalm 68:1–10

*A father to the fatherless, a defender of widows,
is God in his holy dwelling.* Psalm 68:5

When our youngest son joined the Army, we knew that challenges lay ahead. We knew that he would face danger and be tested physically, emotionally, and spiritually. We also knew that in some ways our home would never fully be his home again. In the months leading up to his departure, my wife and I steeled ourselves for these challenges.

Then the day came when Mark had to report. We hugged and said our goodbyes, and then he walked into the recruiting station, leaving me with a moment for which I was decidedly unprepared. The pain of that hard goodbye felt unbearable. At the risk of sounding overly dramatic, I can't remember when I have wept as hard as I did that day. The hard goodbye, and the sense of loss it delivered, cut me to the heart.

In such moments, I am thankful to have a heavenly Father who knows what it is to be separated from a beloved Son. I am thankful to have a God who is described as "a father to the fatherless, a defender of widows" (Psalm 68:5). I believe that if He cares for the orphaned and the widows in their loneliness, He will also care for me and comfort me—even in those moments when I face the struggles that accompany hard goodbyes.

· · ·

Loneliness comes when we forget
about the One who is always with us.

Master Craftsman

Jeremiah 18:1–10

The pot he was shaping from the clay
was marred in his hands; so the potter formed it
into another pot, shaping it as seemed best to him. *Jeremiah 18:4*

When my wife and I were engaged, her dad gave us a special wedding present. As a watchmaker and jeweler, he made our wedding rings. To make my wedding band, Jim used gold scraps left over from resizing other rings—scraps that were seemingly without much value. But in the hands of this craftsman, those pieces became a thing of beauty that I cherish to this day. It is amazing what a master craftsman can do with what others might view as useless.

That is also how God works in our lives. He is the greatest Master Craftsman of all, taking the wasted pieces and broken shards of our lives and restoring them to worth and meaning. The prophet Jeremiah described this when he compared God's work to that of a potter working clay: "The pot he was shaping from the clay was marred in his hands; so the potter formed it into another pot, shaping it as seemed best to him" (Jeremiah 18:4).

No matter what messes we have made of our lives, God can remold us into vessels that are good in His eyes. As we confess any sin and submit ourselves in obedience to His Word, we allow the Master to do His redemptive work in our lives (2 Timothy 2:21). That is the only way for the pieces of our brokenness to be made whole and good once again.

. . .

Broken things can become blessed things
if you let God do the mending.

The Need for Tears

Luke 19:37–44

As [Jesus] approached Jerusalem
and saw the city, he wept over it. *Luke 19:41*

Following the 2010 earthquake in Haiti, we were all overwhelmed by the images of devastation and hardship endured by the people of that tiny nation. Of the many heartbreaking pictures, one captured my attention. It showed a woman staring at the massive destruction— and weeping. Her mind could not process the suffering of her people, and as her heart was crushed, tears poured from her eyes. Her reaction was understandable. Sometimes crying is the only appropriate response to the suffering we encounter.

As I examined that picture, I thought of the compassion of our Lord. Jesus understood the need for tears, and He too wept. But He wept over a different kind of devastation—the destruction brought on by sin. As He drew near to Jerusalem, marked by corruption and injustice and the pain they create, His response was tears. "As he approached Jerusalem and saw the city, he wept over it." (Luke 19:41). Jesus wept out of compassion and grief.

As we encounter the inhumanity, suffering, and sin that wreak havoc in our world, how do we respond? If the heart of Christ breaks over the broken condition of our world, shouldn't ours? And shouldn't we then do everything we can to make a difference for those in need, both spiritually and physically?

• • •

Compassion offers whatever is necessary
to heal the hurts of others.

The Mercy of God

Psalm 31:9–15

Be merciful to me, LORD, for I am in distress; my eyes grow weak with sorrow, my soul and my body with grief. *Psalm 31:9*

It's hard to think about September 11, 2001, without mental images of the destruction, grief, and loss that swept over America and the world following the tragic events of that day. The loss of thousands of lives was compounded by the depth of loss felt corporately—a lost sense of security as a country. The sorrow of loss, personal and corporate, will always accompany the memory of the events of that day.

Those horrific events are not the only painful memories of September 11. It also marks the anniversary of my father-in-law's death. Jim's loss is felt deeply within our family and his circle of friends.

No matter what kind of sorrow we experience, there is only one real comfort—the mercy of God. David, in his own heartache, cried to his heavenly Father, "Be merciful to me, LORD, for I am in distress; my eyes grow weak with sorrow, my soul and my body with grief" (Psalm 31:9). Only in the mercy of God can we find comfort for our pain and peace for our troubled hearts.

In all losses, we can turn to the true Shepherd, Jesus Christ, who alone can heal our brokenness and grief.

• • •

When God permits suffering, He also provides comfort.

The Cost of Fighting

James 4:1–10

What causes fights and quarrels among you? Don't they come
from your desires that battle within you? James 4:1

During a documentary on World War I, the narrator said that if
Britain's casualties in "the war to end all wars" were marched four
abreast past London's war monument, the processional would take
seven days to complete. This staggering word picture set my mind
spinning at the awful cost of war. While those costs include mon-
etary expense, destruction of property, and economic interruption,
none of these compare to the human cost. Both soldiers and civilians
pay the ultimate price, multiplied exponentially by the grief of the
survivors. War is costly.

When believers go to war with one another, the cost is also high.
James wrote, "What causes fights and quarrels among you? Don't
they come from your desires that battle within you?" (James 4:1). In
our own selfish pursuits, we sometimes battle without considering
the price exacted on our witness to the world or our relationships
with one another. Perhaps that is why James preceded these words
with the challenge, "Peacemakers who sow in peace reap a harvest of
righteousness" (3:18).

If we are to represent the Prince of Peace in our world, believers
need to stop fighting with one another and practice peace.

· · ·

When Christians are at peace with one another,
the world can more clearly see the Prince of Peace.

Investing in the Future

Matthew 6:19-24

Store up for yourselves treasures in heaven,
where moths and vermin do not destroy,
and where thieves do not break in and steal. *Matthew 6:20*

Jason Bohn was a college student when he made a hole-in-one golf shot that won him a million dollars. While others may have squandered that money, Bohn had a plan. Wanting to be a pro golfer, he used the money as a living-and-training fund to improve his golf skills. The cash became an investment in his future—an investment that paid off when Bohn won the PGA Tour's 2005 B.C. Open. Bohn's decision to invest in the future instead of living for the moment was a wise one indeed.

In a sense, that is what Jesus calls us to do. We have been entrusted with resources—time, ability, opportunity—and we decide how to use them. Our challenge is to see those resources as an opportunity to invest long-term. "Store up for yourselves treasures in heaven," is how Jesus put it in Matthew 6:20. Those protected treasures cannot be destroyed nor taken away, Jesus assures us.

Think of your resources: talent, time, knowledge. These are temporal and limited. But if you invest them with an eye toward eternity, these temporary things can have enduring impact. What is your focus? Now or forever? Invest in the future. It will not only have an eternal impact but it will also change the way you view life each day.

• • •

The richest people on earth
are those who invest their lives in heaven.

Choices and Consequences

Galatians 6:1–10

Do not be deceived: God cannot be mocked.
A man reaps what he sows. *Galatians 6:7*

In the International Slavery Museum in Liverpool, England, the devastation of generations of enslaved men, women, and children is remembered. The price innocent people have paid for the greed of others is horrific—but theirs is not the only cost. Engraved in a wall of the museum is a profound observation made by Frederick Douglass, former slave and crusader for human rights, which reads, "No man can put a chain about the ankle of his fellow man without at last finding the other end fastened about his own neck." In the act of dehumanizing others, we dehumanize ourselves.

The apostle Paul put it another way when he wrote, "Do not be deceived: God cannot be mocked. A man reaps what he sows" (Galatians 6:7). Paul's words form a stark reminder to us that our choices have consequences—and that includes how we choose to treat others. When we choose to hate, that hate can return to us in the form of consequences that we can never fully prepare for. We can find ourselves alienated from others, angry with ourselves, and hamstrung in our ability to serve Christ effectively.

Instead, let's choose "not [to] become weary in doing good, for at the proper time we will reap a harvest. . . . As we have opportunity, let us do good to all people" (vv. 9–10).

• • •

The seeds we sow today
determine the kind of fruit we'll reap tomorrow.

Yet I Will Rejoice

Habakkuk 3:11-19

Yet I will rejoice in the LORD,
I will be joyful in God my Savior. *Habakkuk 3:18*

Life in our world can be difficult. At some point, most of us have wondered, *Where is God in my trouble?* And we may have thought, *It seems like injustice is winning and God is silent.* We have a choice as to how we respond to our troubles. The prophet Habakkuk had an attitude worth following: He made the choice to rejoice.

Habakkuk saw the rapid increase in Judah's moral and spiritual failings, and this disturbed him deeply. But God's response troubled him even more. God would use the wicked nation of Babylon to punish Judah. Habakkuk did not fully understand this, but he could rejoice because he had learned to rely on the wisdom, justice, and sovereignty of God. He concluded his book with a wonderful affirmation: "Yet I will rejoice in the LORD, I will be joyful in God my Savior" (3:18). Though it was not clear how Judah would survive, Habakkuk had learned to trust God amid injustice, suffering, and loss. He would live by his faith in God alone. With this kind of faith came joy in God, despite the circumstances surrounding him.

We too can rejoice in our trials, have surefooted confidence in God, and live on the heights of His sovereignty.

• • •

Praising God in our trials turns burdens into blessings.

Regaining Our Balance

Ephesians 6:10–18

Put on the full armor of God, so that when the day of evil comes, you may be able to stand your ground. Ephesians 6:13

For the last few years, my wife, Marlene, has suffered from inner ear problems that cause her to lose her equilibrium. Without warning, something inside her ear is upset and she becomes dizzy. If she tries to sit or stand, a condition called vertigo makes that impossible—and she has to lie down. No amount of effort can compensate for the power of the inner ear to disrupt and disturb. An active person, Marlene finds these unwelcome episodes frustrating.

Sometimes life is like that. Something unexpected upsets our routine, and we are knocked off-balance. Perhaps it's bad news about our job being eliminated or disturbing test results from our doctor. It may even be an attack from our spiritual enemy. In each case, our emotional equilibrium is hammered, and we feel as if we can't stand.

Those moments should cause us to turn to God. When we feel we are losing our balance, He can help. He provides spiritual resources to help us stand. Paul says, "Put on the full armor of God, so that when the day of evil comes, you may be able to stand your ground" (Ephesians 6:13).

When life knocks us off our feet, we don't have to be frustrated. With God's strength lifting us up and God's armor protecting us, we can still stand strong.

• • •

We can endure anything if we depend on God for everything.

Help Needed

Hebrews 4:9–16

Let us then approach God's throne of grace
with confidence, so that we may receive mercy
and find grace to help us in our time of need. *Hebrews 4:16*

During World War II, the British Isles represented the last line of resistance against the sweep of Nazi oppression in Europe. Under relentless attack and in danger of collapse, however, Britain lacked the resources to see the conflict through to victory. For that reason, British Prime Minister Winston Churchill went on BBC radio and appealed to the world: "Give us the tools, and we will finish the job." He knew that without help from the outside, they could not endure the assault they were facing.

Life is like that. Often, we are inadequate for the troubles life throws at us, and we need help from outside of ourselves. As members of the body of Christ, that help can come at times from our Christian brothers and sisters (Romans 12:10–13)—and that is a wonderful thing. Ultimately, however, we seek help from our heavenly Father. The good and great news is that our God has invited us to come confidently before Him: "Let us then approach God's throne of grace with confidence, so that we may receive mercy and find grace to help us in our time of need" (Hebrews 4:16).

At such times, our greatest resource is prayer—for it brings us into the very presence of God. There we find, in His mercy and grace, the help we need.

• • •

Don't let prayer be your last recourse
in time of need; make it your first.

Long-Awaited Reunion

1 Thessalonians 4:13–18

We who are still alive and are left will be caught up together with them in the clouds to meet the Lord in the air. 1 Thessalonians 4:17

As a boy, I had a collie named Prince Boy, a great dog that I really loved. One day, he disappeared. I didn't know if he had been stolen or if he had simply run away—but I was devastated. I searched everywhere. In fact, one of my earliest childhood memories is of climbing a tall tree from which I could scan our neighborhood in hopes of spotting him. I desperately wanted my beloved dog back. For weeks, I was always watching and hoping to see Prince Boy again. But we were never reunited.

There's an infinitely greater sense of loss when we think we'll never again see a loved one who dies. But for those who know and love the Lord, death's parting is only temporary. One day we will be reunited forever!

Paul assured the Thessalonians, "The dead in Christ will rise first. After that, we who are alive and are left will be caught up together with them in the clouds to meet the Lord in the air. And so we will be with the Lord forever" (1 Thessalonians 4:16–17). The words that provide comfort to the grieving heart are *together* and *we*. These words of reunion indicate that followers of Christ don't ever have to experience permanent separation.

For us, death is not a goodbye; it's a "see you later."

• • •

God's people never say goodbye for the last time.

Enemy Deceptions

John 8:42–47

I am afraid that just as Eve was deceived by the serpent's cunning,
your minds may somehow be led astray from your sincere
and pure devotion to Christ. *2 Corinthians 11:3*

Written in the sixth century BC by Chinese general Sun Tzu, *The Art of War* has been a guide for military thinking for centuries. But it has also been used by men and women in a wide variety of other arenas, including leadership, management, business, politics, and sports. What Sun Tzu wrote about military warfare can help followers of Christ to understand the tactics of our spiritual enemy: "All warfare is based on deception. Hence, when able to attack, we must seem unable; when using our forces, we must seem inactive; when we are near, we must make the enemy believe we are far away; when far away, we must make him believe we are near."

Likewise, the spiritual warfare that Satan wages against us is also based on deceit. In fact, the very first sin was the result of the enemy's deception. Notice what Paul said: "I am afraid that just as Eve was deceived by the serpent's cunning, your minds may somehow be led astray from your sincere and pure devotion to Christ" (2 Corinthians 11:3).

This truth is what gives such importance to our Lord's warning that Satan is the father of lies (John 8:44), ever seeking to deceive us. What is our defense? To saturate our hearts in the truth of God's Word. Only God's inspired truth can protect us against the deceptions of the enemy.

• • •

God's truth is the best protection against Satan's lies.

Totally Clean

1 John 1:1–10

*If we confess our sins, he is faithful and just and will forgive us
our sins and purify us from all unrighteousness.* 1 John 1:9

A friend was updating me on his past year—a year in which he had been receiving ongoing medical treatment for cancer. The smile on his face was a powerful testimony to the good news he had just received. He said that at his one-year checkup the doctor announced that the test results all pointed to one thing: "You are totally clean!" What a difference two words can make! To my friend, "totally clean" meant every trace of the disease that had threatened his life only months before had been wiped from his body. We rejoiced to hear that he was totally clean!

King David, after his moral failure with Bathsheba, longed for a similar thing to happen in his heart. Hoping for the stains of his sin to be washed away, he cried out, "Create in me a pure heart, O God, and renew a steadfast spirit within me" (Psalm 51:10). The good news for him and for us is that our sins can be taken care of. When we need cleansing, John's familiar words bring hope: "If we confess our sins, he is faithful and just and will forgive us our sins and purify us from all unrighteousness" (1 John 1:9).

We can't cleanse our own hearts; only God can do that. If we confess our sins to Him, He promises to make us totally clean!

• • •

Confession to God always brings cleansing from God.

The New Normal

Hebrews 4:9–16

For we do not have a high priest who is unable to empathize with
our weaknesses, but we have one who has been tempted
in every way, just as we are—yet he did not sin. *Hebrews 4:15*

A pastor who was trained in trauma and grief counseling commented that the greatest challenge for people who are hurting is often not the immediate heartache of the loss. Instead, the biggest problem is adjusting to the different kind of life that follows. What once was normal may never be normal again. So the challenge for those offering help is to assist the sufferers as they establish the "new normal." It may be a new normal that no longer includes robust health, a treasured relationship, or a satisfying job. Or it may be living without a loved one who has been taken in death. The gravity of such a loss forces us to live a different kind of life—no matter how unwelcome it may be.

When our "new normal" comes, it's easy to think no one understands how we feel. But that isn't true. Part of the reason Jesus came was to experience life among us, resulting in His present ministry: "For we do not have a high priest who is unable to empathize with our weaknesses, but we have one who has been tempted in every way, just as we are—yet he did not sin" (Hebrews 4:15).

Our Savior lived a perfect life, yet He also knew the pains of a broken world. He endured sorrow; He suffered agony. And He stands ready to encourage us when the dark moments of life force us to embrace a new normal.

• • •

In our desert of grief, Jesus can provide an oasis of hope.

Flying Solo

John 14:15–27

Don't you know that you yourselves are God's temple
and that God's Spirit dwells in your midst? *1 Corinthians 3:16*

May 21, 1927, marked a turning point in aviation history as Charles Lindbergh completed the first-ever solo, nonstop, trans-Atlantic flight. There had been other flights across the Atlantic, but none were accomplished by a pilot flying alone. It was a historic achievement. When Lindbergh landed at Le Bourget Field in Paris, he was thronged by thousands of admirers applauding his success. And when he returned to America, he was further honored with parades and awards in celebration of his individualistic courage and spirit.

Even though Lindbergh's solo flight was dangerous, living in this fallen world of ours can be far more so. Followers of Christ, however, can be encouraged and comforted that we never have to "fly solo." The night before His crucifixion, Jesus promised that He would not abandon us but would send His Spirit to be with us and in us (John 14:16–17). The apostle Paul later affirmed this, saying, "Don't you know that you yourselves are God's temple and that God's Spirit dwells in your midst?" (1 Corinthians 3:16).

In a world filled with despair and trouble, we can take courage. The Holy Spirit lives within us, providing us with His peace and comfort (John 14:26–27). Aren't you thankful that you never have to fly solo?

• • •

The Spirit within us guarantees that we're never alone.

Wake-Up Call

1 Peter 5:1–9

Be alert and of sober mind. Your enemy the devil prowls around like a roaring lion looking for someone to devour. *1 Peter 5:8*

One early autumn morning as I drove to work in the dark, I was startled by a flash of brown in my headlights followed by the sound of something hitting the front of my car. I had clipped a deer at seventy miles per hour! It was only a glancing blow, and no damage was done to my car (or the deer, as far as I could tell), but it really shook me up. I had been in my usual "autopilot mode" for the familiar drive to the office, but the shock of the incident certainly got my attention. I was now fully alert and trying to calm a racing heartbeat. It was a most unpleasant wake-up call.

The apostle Peter offers us a different kind of wake-up call—one that while unpleasant is necessary. He alerts us to a spiritual battle we are engaged in with a powerful enemy. Peter warns, "Be alert and of sober mind. Your enemy the devil prowls around like a roaring lion looking for someone to devour" (1 Peter 5:8). This is a call to wake up, see the danger, and be ready for his attack!

Only when we are aware of the danger that faces us every day will we consciously seek the help we need. And only if we are on the alert will we lean on the strength of our Lord, who is greater than our spiritual enemy.

• • •

The Christian life is a battleground.

Faithful unto Death

Revelation 2:8–11

Do not be afraid of what you are about to suffer. . . .
Be faithful, even to the point of death,
and I will give you life as your victor's crown. *Revelation 2:10*

The Walker Art Gallery in Liverpool, England, has a painting of a Roman soldier faithfully standing guard in ancient Pompeii. The painting was inspired by an archaeological discovery in Pompeii of an ashen-encased Roman soldier in full military gear. The volcanic eruption of Mount Vesuvius in AD 79 covered that city in lava, capturing the people and their culture in a moment of time. The painting *Faithful unto Death* is a testimony to the sentinel's continuing vigil even as his world was being engulfed in fiery death.

The church at Smyrna—a first-century congregation that suffered persecution for Christ—was challenged to be faithful unto death. Their spiritual commitment had not gone unnoticed by the Master (Revelation 2:9). And for the suffering that was to come, Jesus offered this encouragement: "Do not be afraid of what you are about to suffer. I tell you, the devil will put some of you in prison to test you. . . . Be faithful, even to the point of death, and I will give you life as your victor's crown" (v. 10).

The Lord understands what we are going through now and what we will face in the future. Though there's suffering in this world, He promises eternal life to His children. In His strength we can be faithful unto death (Philippians 4:12–13).

• • •

Our faith may be tested so that we may trust His faithfulness.

Falling Short

Romans 3:19–28

All have sinned and fall short of the glory of God. Romans 3:23

One of the fads of 1970s America was the motorcycle jump. This trend reached its high (and low) point on September 8, 1974. Thousands of spectators gathered around the Snake River Canyon in Idaho to see if Evel Knievel could jump across the chasm in a specially designed "sky cycle." In the end, however, it was unsuccessful. Knievel made it only part of the way across the gulf before his parachute deployed, and he dropped to the canyon floor below. Some spectators asked, "How far across the canyon did he get?" But that wasn't the point. He didn't make it all the way across, so he fell short of his goal.

This scene is a good illustration of sin. The Bible talks about sin in Romans 3:23, where Paul declared, "For all have sinned and fall short of the glory of God." No one is capable of bridging the gap between God and ourselves by our own efforts, but the Savior came to do just that on our behalf. Christ perfectly fulfilled God's standards, then gave His life on the cross to pay for our failure and wrongdoing. Where we could only fall short, Christ's work, offered in love, accomplished all that was needed.

Our response is to trust Him and receive this matchless gift of salvation.

• • •

The cross of Christ bridges the gap
we could never cross on our own.

The Trail of Tears

Revelation 21:1–7

"[God] will wipe every tear from their eyes.
There will be no more death" or mourning or crying. *Revelation 21:4*

A very severe and tragic event in US history was the forced relocation of thousands of Native Americans in the early nineteenth century. Native American tribes, who had struck treaties with and fought alongside the burgeoning white population, were driven out of their ancestral lands. In the winter of 1838, thousands of Cherokee were forced to embark on a brutal 1,000-mile march westward known as the Trail of Tears. This injustice resulted in the deaths of thousands of people, many of whom had little or no clothing, shoes, or supplies for such a journey.

The world continues to be filled with injustice, pain, and heartache. And many today may feel as if they are leaving a trail of tears—tears that go unnoticed and grief that is not comforted. But our Lord sees our tears and comforts our weary hearts (2 Corinthians 1:3–5). He also declares the hope of a future time not marked by the stains of sin or injustice. In that day and in that place, God "'will wipe every tear from their eyes. There will be no more death' or sorrow or crying or pain, for the old order of things has passed away" (Revelation 21:4).

The God who offers freedom from tears in the future is the only One who can fully comfort our tears now.

• • •

When God permits trials, He also provides comfort.

No Simple Recipe

Hebrews 4:11–16

*For we do not have a high priest who is unable
to empathize with our weaknesses, but we have one
who has been tempted in every way, just as we are.* Hebrews 4:15

For our grandson's birthday, my wife baked and decorated a gigantic chocolate chip cookie to serve at his party. She got out her cookbook, gathered the ingredients, and began to follow the basic steps involved in making cookies. She followed a simple recipe and everything turned out well.

Wouldn't it be nice if life was like that? Just follow a few easy steps and then enjoy a happy life.

But life is not so simple. We live in a fallen world, and there is no easy recipe to follow that will ensure a life free of pain, loss, injustice, or suffering.

In the midst of life's pain, we need the personal care of the Savior who lived in this world and experienced the same struggles we face. Hebrews 4:15 encourages us: "For we do not have a high priest who is unable to empathize with our weaknesses, but we have one who has been tempted in every way, just as we are." Christ, who died to give us life, is completely sufficient to carry us through our heartaches and dark experiences. He "took up our pain and bore our suffering" (Isaiah 53:4).

Jesus knows there is no simple "recipe" to prevent the heartaches of life, so He entered into them with us. Will we trust Him with our tears and grief?

• • •

The Christ who died to give us life
will carry us through its heartaches.

Refreshing Candor

John 4:7–26

Whoever looks intently into the perfect law
that gives freedom, and continues in it, . . .
they will be blessed in what they do. *James 1:25*

Of the many things I love about my mom, chief among them may be her candor. Many times I have called to ask her opinion on a matter and she has consistently responded, "Don't ask my opinion unless you want to hear it. I'm not going to try to figure out what you want to hear. I'll tell you what I really think."

In a world where words are carefully parsed, her straightforwardness is refreshing. It is also one of the characteristics of a true friend. Real friends speak the truth to us in love—even if it isn't what we want to hear. As the proverb says, "Wounds from a friend can be trusted" (Proverbs 27:6).

This is one of the reasons Jesus is the greatest of friends. When He encountered the woman at the well (John 4:7–26), He refused to be pulled into a tug-of-war over secondary issues but instead drove to the deepest issues and needs of her heart. He challenged her about the character of the Father and lovingly spoke to her of her broken dreams and deep disappointments.

As we walk with our Lord, may we allow Him to speak candidly to the true condition of our hearts through the Scriptures—that we might turn to Him and find His grace to help us in our times of need.

• • •

Jesus always tells us truth.

Broken Bones

Psalm 51:1–13

Let me hear joy and gladness;
let the bones you have crushed rejoice. *Psalm 51:8*

Years ago, I played collegiate soccer as a goalkeeper. It was more fun than I can describe here, but all that fun came at a hefty price—one I continue to pay today. Being a goalie means that you are constantly throwing your body into harm's way to prevent the other team from scoring, often resulting in injuries. During the course of one season, I suffered a broken leg, several cracked ribs, a separated shoulder, and a concussion! Today, especially on cold days, I am visited by painful reminders of those broken bones.

David also had reminders of broken bones, but his injuries were spiritual, not physical. After David's moral collapse involving an affair with Bathsheba and the murder of her husband, God firmly disciplined him. But then David turned to Him in repentance and prayed, "Let me hear joy and gladness; let the bones you have crushed rejoice" (Psalm 51:8).

God's chastening was so crushing that David felt like his bones were broken. Yet he trusted that the God of grace could both repair his brokenness and rekindle his joy. In our own failure and sin, it's a comfort to know that God loves us enough to pursue us and restore us with His loving discipline.

• • •

God's hand of discipline is a hand of love.

Unseen Danger

James 1:13–25

Each one is tempted when he is drawn away
by his own desires and enticed. James 1:14 NKJV

When I was a young child, our family escaped near tragedy. Most of the main appliances in the house, as well as the furnace, were fueled by natural gas, but a small leak in one of the gas lines put our lives at risk. As the gas poured into our little house, our family was overcome by the lethal fumes and we lost consciousness. Had we not been discovered by a neighbor who happened to stop by for a visit, we all could have been killed by this dangerous, unseen enemy.

As followers of Christ, we can also find ourselves surrounded by unseen dangers. The toxic realities of temptation and the weaknesses of our own human frailty can endanger our lives and relationships. Unlike the natural gas in my childhood home, however, these unseen dangers do not come from outside of us—they reside within us. James wrote, "Each one is tempted when he is drawn away by his own desires and enticed" (James 1:14 NKJV).

Our natural tendency to sin, compounded by blind spots that prevent us from seeing our own weaknesses, can lead to toxic choices that ruin us. It is only by submitting to God as He shows us our hearts in His Word (vv. 23–25) that we can live a life that pleases the Master.

• • •

The unseen Spirit of God is the greatest protection
against sin's unseen dangers.

Flight Simulator

John 16:25–33

I have told you these things,
so that in me you may have peace. *John 16:33*

When airplane pilots are training, they spend many hours in flight simulators. These simulators give the students a chance to experience the challenges and dangers of flying an aircraft—but without the risk. The pilots don't have to leave the ground, and if they crash in the simulation, they can calmly walk away.

Simulators are tremendous teaching tools—helpful in preparing the aspiring pilot to take command of an actual aircraft. The devices, however, have a shortcoming. They create an artificial experience in which the full-blown pressures of handling a real cockpit cannot be fully replicated.

Real life is like that, isn't it? It cannot be simulated. There is no risk-free environment in which we can experience life's ups and downs unharmed. The risks and dangers of living in a broken world are inescapable. That's why the words of Jesus are reassuring. He said, "I have told you these things, so that in me you may have peace. In this world you will have trouble. But take heart! I have overcome the world" (John 16:33).

Although we can't avoid the dangers of life in a fallen world, we can have peace through a relationship with Jesus. He has secured our ultimate victory.

• • •

No life is more secure than a life surrendered to God.

Unfailing Mercy

Luke 22:54–62

Because of the LORD's great love
we are not consumed, for his compassions never fail. . . .
Great is your faithfulness. *Lamentations 3:22–23*

As I strolled through Chicago's O'Hare Airport, something caught my eye—a hat worn by someone racing through the concourse. What caught my attention was the message it conveyed in just two words: "Deny Everything." I wondered what it meant. Don't ever admit to guilt? Or deny yourself the pleasures and luxuries of life? I scratched my head at the mystery of those two simple words, "Deny Everything."

One of Jesus's followers, Simon Peter, did some denying. In a critical moment, he denied three times that He even knew Jesus! (Luke 22:57, 58, 60). His fear-filled act of denial caused him such guilt and heartache that, broken by his spiritual failure, he wandered off and weep bitterly (v. 62).

But Peter's denial of Christ, like our own moments of spiritual denial, could never diminish the compassion of God. The prophet Jeremiah wrote, "Because of the LORD's great love we are not consumed, for his compassions never fail. They are new every morning; great is your faithfulness" (Lamentations 3:22–23). We can take heart that even when we fail, our faithful God comes to us in mercy and compassion that never fails!

• • •

Being imperfect emphasizes our dependence on God's mercy.

The Path of Wisdom

Psalm 38:1–15

LORD, I wait for you; you will answer, Lord my God. *Psalm 38:15*

A quote sometimes attributed to Albert Einstein goes like this: "Only two things are infinite, the universe and human stupidity, and I'm not sure about the former." Sadly, it does seem that far too often there is no limit to the foolishness we get ourselves into—or the damage we create by our foolishness and the choices it fosters.

It was in such a season of regret that King David poured out his struggle and complaint to God in Psalm 38. As he recounted his own failings, as well as the painful consequences he was enduring because of those failings, the shepherd-king made an insightful comment: "My wounds fester and are loathsome because of my sinful folly" (v. 5). Although the psalmist does not give us the details of those choices or of his worsening wounds, one thing is clear—David recognized his own foolishness as their root cause.

The answer for such destructive foolishness is to embrace the wisdom of God. Proverbs 9:10 reminds us, "The fear of the LORD is the beginning of wisdom, and the knowledge of the Holy One is understanding." Only by allowing God to transform us can we overcome the foolish decisions that cause so much trouble. With His loving guidance, we can follow the pathway of godly wisdom.

• • •

God's wisdom is given to those who humbly ask Him for it.

Be Still

Psalm 46

*Be still, and know that I am God; I will be exalted
among the nations, I will be exalted in the earth.* Psalm 46:10

Eric Liddell, memorialized in the movie *Chariots of Fire*, won a gold medal in the 1924 Paris Olympics before going to China as a missionary. Some years later, with the outbreak of World War II, Liddell sent his family to safety in Canada, but he remained in China. Soon Liddell and other foreign missionaries were interned in a Japanese detainment camp. After months of captivity, he developed what doctors feared was a brain tumor.

Every Sunday afternoon a band would play near the hospital, so one day Liddell requested they play the hymn "Be Still, My Soul." As he listened, I wonder if Eric pondered these words from the song: "Be still, my soul: the hour is hastening on / When we shall be forever with the Lord. / When disappointment, grief, and fear are gone, / Sorrow forgot, love's purest joys restored. /Be still, my soul: when change and tears are past / All safe and blessed we shall meet at last."

That beautiful hymn, so comforting to Eric as he faced an illness that led to his death three days later, expresses a great reality of Scripture. In Psalm 46:10, David wrote, "Be still, and know that I am God." In our darkest moments, we can rest, for our Lord conquered death on our behalf. Be still, and allow Him to calm your greatest fears.

• • •

God's whisper of comfort quiets the noise of our trials.

Embarrassing Moments

John 8:1–11

*"Neither do I condemn you," Jesus declared.
"Go now and leave your life of sin." John 8:11*

The flashing lights of the police car drew my attention to a motorist who had been pulled over for a traffic violation. As the officer, ticket book in hand, walked back to his car, I could clearly see the embarrassed driver sitting helplessly behind the wheel of her car. With her hands, she attempted to block her face from the view of passersby—hoping to hide her identity. Her actions were a reminder to me of how embarrassing it can be when we are exposed by our choices and their consequences.

When a guilty woman was brought before Jesus and her immorality was exposed, the crowd did more than just watch. They called for her condemnation, but Jesus showed mercy. The only One with the right to judge sin responded to her failure with compassion. After dispatching her accusers, "Neither do I condemn you," Jesus declared. "Go now and leave your life of sin" (John 8:11). His compassion reminds us of His forgiving grace, and His command to her points to His great desire that we live in the joy of that grace. Both elements show the depth of Christ's concern for us when we stumble and fall.

Even in our most embarrassing moments of failure, we can cry out to Him and find that His grace is truly amazing.

• • •

Jesus alone can supply the grace we need for each trial we face.

Mixed Emotions

Psalm 73:23–26

Even in laughter the heart may ache,
and rejoicing may end in grief. Proverbs 14:13

For Marlene and me, "mixed emotions" precisely describes our wedding. Don't take that the wrong way. It was a wonderful event that we continue to celebrate more than forty years later. The wedding celebration, however, was dampened because Marlene's mom died of cancer just weeks before. Marlene's aunt was a wonderful stand-in as the "mother of the bride," but in the midst of our happiness, something clearly wasn't right. Mom was missing, and that affected everything.

That experience typifies life in a broken world. Our experiences here are a mixed bag of good and bad, joy and pain—a reality that Solomon expressed when he wrote, "Even in laughter the heart may ache, and rejoicing may end in grief" (Proverbs 14:13). The merry heart often does grieve, for that is what this life sometimes demands.

Thankfully, however, this life is not all there is. And in the life that is to come, those who know Christ have a promise: "'He will wipe every tear from their eyes. There will be no more death' or mourning or crying or pain, for the old order of things has passed away" (Revelation 21:4). In that great day, there will be no mixed emotions—only hearts filled with the presence of God!

• • •

For the Christian, the dark sorrows of earth
will one day be changed into the bright songs of heaven.

Load Line

1 Peter 5:5–9

Humble yourselves, therefore, under God's mighty hand,
that he may lift you up in due time. Cast all your anxiety on him
because he cares for you. 1 Peter 5:6–7

In the nineteenth century, ships were often recklessly overloaded, resulting in those ships going down and the crews being lost at sea. In 1875, to remedy this negligent practice, British politician Samuel Plimsoll led the charge for legislation to create a line on the side of a ship to show if it was carrying too much cargo. That "load line" became known as the Plimsoll Line, and it continues to mark the hulls of ships today.

Sometimes, like those ships, our lives can seem overloaded with fears, struggles, and heartaches. We can even feel that we are in danger of going under. In those times, however, it is reassuring to remember that we have a remarkable resource. We have a heavenly Father who stands ready to help us carry that load. The apostle Peter said, "Humble yourselves, therefore, under God's mighty hand, that he may lift you up in due time. Cast all your anxiety on him because he cares for you" (1 Peter 5:6–7). He is capable of handling the cares that overwhelm us.

Though the testings of life may feel like a burden too heavy to bear, we can have full assurance that our heavenly Father loves us deeply and knows our load limits. Whatever we face, He will help us to endure.

. . .

God may lead us into troubled waters to deepen our trust in Him.

Guidance Needed

John 16:13–17

When he, the Spirit of truth, comes,
he will guide you into all the truth. John 16:13

St. Nicholas's Collegiate Church in Galway, Ireland, has both a long history and an active present. It's the oldest church in Ireland, and it provides guidance in a very practical way. The church towers over the town, and its steeple is used by ships' captains as a guide for navigating their way safely into Galway Bay. For centuries, this church has reliably pointed the way home for sailors.

We can all certainly identify with the need for guidance. In fact, Jesus addressed this very need during His Upper Room Discourse. He said that after His departure the Holy Spirit would play a crucial role in the lives of believers. As part of that role, Jesus promised, "When he, the Spirit of truth comes, he will guide you into all the truth" (John 16:13).

What a marvelous provision! In a world of confusion and fear, guidance is often needed. We can easily be misdirected by the culture around us or by the brokenness within us (1 John 2:15–17). God's Spirit, however, is here to help, to direct, and to guide. How thankful we can be that the Spirit of truth has come to give us the guidance that we often so desperately need. Set your course by His life, and you will reach safe harbor.

• • •

The Spirit is a reliable guide in all of life's seas.

The Power of Music

Psalm 59:6–16

I will sing of your strength, in the morning I will sing of your love;
you are my fortress, my refuge in times of trouble. *Psalm 59:16*

In Wales, the music of men's chorus groups is deeply engrained in the culture. Prior to World War II, one Welsh glee club had a friendly yet competitive rivalry with a German glee club, but that bond was replaced with animosity during and after the war. The tension was gradually overcome, though, by the message on the trophy shared by the two choruses: "Speak with me, and you're my friend. Sing with me, and you're my brother."

The power of music to heal and help is a gift from God that comforts many. Perhaps that is why the Psalms speak so deeply to us. There we find lyrics that connect with our hearts, allowing us to speak to God from the depth of our spirits. "I will sing of your strength, in the morning I will sing of your love; you are my fortress, my refuge in times of trouble" (Psalm 59:16). Amazingly, David wrote this song as he was being hunted down by men seeking to kill him! Despite his circumstances, David remembered God's power and mercy, and singing of them encouraged him to go on.

May our God give us a song today that will remind us of His goodness and greatness, no matter what we may face.

• • •

I will make music to the LORD, the God of Israel. —Judges 5:3 NLT

Prone to Wander

Psalm 119:9–16

I seek you with all my heart; do not let me stray
from your commands. *Psalm 119:10*

One of my favorite classic hymns is "Come, Thou Fount of Every Blessing," which was written in 1757 by twenty-two-year-old Robert Robinson. In the hymn's lyrics is a line that always captures my attention and forces me to do some self-evaluation. The line says, "Prone to wander, Lord, I feel it. Prone to leave the God I love." I feel that way sometimes. Too often I find myself distracted and drifting instead of having my heart and mind focused on the Savior who loves me and gave himself for me. Robert Robinson and I are not alone in this.

In those seasons of wandering, our heart of hearts doesn't want to drift from God—but like Paul, we often do what we don't want to do (Romans 7:19), and we desperately need to turn back to the Shepherd of our heart who can draw us to himself. David wrote of this struggle in his great anthem to the Scriptures, Psalm 119, saying, "I seek you with all my heart; do not let me stray from your commands" (v. 10).

Sometimes, even when our hearts long to seek God, the distractions of life can draw us away from Him and His Word. How grateful we can be for a patient, compassionate heavenly Father whose grace is always sufficient—even when we are prone to wander!

•   •   •

Our tendency to wander is matched
by God's willingness to pursue.

You've Got a Friend

Psalm 23

[Jesus said,] "I have called you friends." *John 15:15*

One of the ironic consequences of the sweeping growth of social media is that we often find ourselves more personally isolated. One online article warns: "Those who oppose leading one's life primarily or exclusively online claim that virtual friends are not adequate substitutes for real-world friends, and . . . individuals who substitute virtual friends for physical friends become even lonelier and more depressive than before."

Technology aside, all of us battle with seasons of loneliness, wondering if anyone knows, understands, or cares about the burdens we carry or the struggles we face. But followers of Christ have an assurance that brings comfort to our weary hearts. The comforting presence of the Savior is promised in words that are undeniable, for the psalmist David wrote, "Even though I walk through the darkest valley, I will fear no evil, for you are with me; your rod and your staff, they comfort me" (Psalm 23:4).

Whether isolated by our own choices, by the cultural trends that surround us, or by the painful losses of life, all who know Christ can rest in the presence of the Shepherd of our hearts. What a friend we have in Jesus!

• • •

Those who know Jesus as their Friend are never alone.

Slow Healing Process

Revelation 21:1–8

> "He will wipe every tear from their eyes. There will be
> no more death" or mourning or crying or pain,
> for the old order of things has passed away. *Revelation 21:4*

Just four weeks after our son Mark joined the US Army, he injured his knee seriously in a training exercise. As a result, he was released from the military. So, at age nineteen, he had to use a cane to get around for a while. Because of the severity of the injury, he endured two years of recovery, rest, and rehab. Finally, Mark was able to set aside the knee braces he had worn since the accident. Although he still experiences residual pain, the long, slow healing process has brought him back to full use of his leg.

Physical healing is often much slower than we anticipate. This is true of spiritual healing as well. The consequences of unwise choices or the actions of hurtful people can create burdens or wounds that endure for a lifetime. But for the child of God, there is hope. Although full restoration is not always experienced in this life, the promise of healing is sure. The apostle John wrote, "'He will wipe every tear from their eyes. There will be no more death' or mourning or crying or pain, for the old order of things has passed away" (Revelation 21:4).

In our seasons of pain, it is comforting to know that eventually, in His awesome presence, we will be whole forever.

• • •

When we come to Christ in our brokenness, He makes us whole.

Forgotten Memories

Psalm 103:1–8

Praise the LORD, my soul, and forget not all his benefits. *Psalm 103:2*

Recently, a friend from my youth emailed me a picture of our junior high track team. The grainy black-and-white snapshot showed a vaguely familiar group of teens with our two coaches. I was instantly swept back in time to happy memories of running the mile and the half-mile in track meets. Yet even as I enjoyed remembering those days, I found myself thinking about how easily I had forgotten them and moved on to other things.

As we make our way on the journey of life, it is easy to forget places, people, and events that have been important to us along the way. Time passes, yesterday fades, and we become obsessed with the concerns of the moment. When this happens, we can also forget just how good God has been to us. Perhaps that is why David remembered as he wrote, "Praise the LORD, my soul; all my inmost being, praise his holy name. Praise the LORD, my soul, and forget not all his benefits" (Psalm 103:1–2).

Never is this remembrance more needed than when the heartaches of life crowd in on us. When we are feeling overwhelmed and forgotten, it's important to recall everything He has done for us. In remembering, we find the encouragement to trust Him in the present and for the future.

•   •   •

Remembering God's faithfulness in the past
strengthens us for the future.

The Big Comeback

1 John 1

If we confess our sins, he is faithful and just and will forgive us our sins and purify us from all unrighteousness. 1 John 1:9

Chad Pennington is a former American football player who suffered multiple career-threatening injuries. Twice, his injuries forced him to endure surgery, months of physical therapy, and weeks of training to get back onto the field. Yet, both times he not only returned to playing but he also excelled at such a high level that he was named Comeback Player of the Year in the National Football League. For Pennington, his efforts were an expression of his determination to return to football.

Spiritually, when sin and failure break our relationship with God and sideline our service, determination alone is not what restores us to rightness with God and usefulness in His kingdom. When we are sidelined because of sin, the path to a comeback is confession as well. "If we confess our sins, he is faithful and just and will forgive us our sins and purify us from all unrighteousness" (1 John 1:9).

For us to be able to recover from our spiritual failings, we are absolutely dependent on the One who gave himself for us. And that gives us hope. Christ, who died for us, loves us with an everlasting love and will respond with grace as we confess our faults to Him. Through confession, we can find His gracious restoration—the greatest of all comebacks.

• • •

Confession is the path that leads to restoration.

Lasting Regrets

Psalm 32:1–7

> When I kept silent, my bones wasted away
> through my groaning all day long. *Psalm 32:3*

While I was talking with a gifted pianist, she asked me if I played any musical instruments. When I responded, "I play the radio," she laughed and asked if I had ever wanted to play any instrument. My embarrassed answer was, "I took piano lessons as a boy but gave it up." Now, in my adult years, I regret not continuing with the piano. I love music and wish I could play today. That conversation was a fresh reminder to me that life is often constituted by the choices we make—and some of them produce regret.

Some choices produce much more serious and painful regrets. King David discovered this when he chose to sleep with another man's wife and then killed that man. He described the guilt that filled him as devastating, saying, "When I kept silent, my bones wasted away through my groaning all day long. For day and night your hand was heavy on me; my strength was sapped as in the heat of summer" (Psalm 32:3–4). But David acknowledged and confessed his sin to God and found forgiveness (v. 5).

It is only from God that we can receive the grace of forgiveness when our choices have produced painful regrets. And only in Him do we find the wisdom to make better choices.

• • •

God's forgiveness frees us from the chains of regret.

A Matter of Trust

Psalm 5

> Let all who take refuge in you be glad; let them ever sing for joy.
> Spread your protection over them. *Psalm 5:11*

A news item from Australia told the story of Pascale Honore, a paraplegic woman who, after eighteen years of being in a wheelchair, has taken up surfing. How?

Ty Swan, a young surfer, straps her to his back with duct tape. After getting the balance perfect, Ty paddles out into the ocean so they can catch a wave and Pascale can experience the exhilaration of surfing. This requires a tremendous amount of trust; so many things could go wrong. Yet her confidence in Ty is enough to enable her to enjoy a dream come true, in spite of the danger.

Life is like that for the follower of Christ. We live in a dangerous world, filled with unpredictable challenges and unseen perils. Yet, we have joy because we know Someone who is strong enough to carry us through the churning waves of life that threaten to overwhelm us. The psalmist wrote, "Let all who take refuge in you be glad; let them ever sing for joy. Spread your protection over them, that those who love your name may rejoice in you" (Psalm 5:11).

In the face of life's great dangers and challenges, we can know a joy borne out of our trust in God. His strength is more than enough!

• • •

Our faith is stretched by exchanging
our weakness for God's strength.

A Sanctuary

Matthew 11:25–30

Come to me, all you who are weary and burdened,
and I will give you rest. Matthew 11:28

Entering a church in Klang, Malaysia, I was intrigued by the sign welcoming us into the building. It declared the place to be "A Sanctuary for the Heavy Laden."

Few things better reflect the heart of Christ than for His church to be a place where burdens are lifted and the weary find rest. This was vital in Jesus's ministry, for He said, "Come to me, all you who are weary and burdened, and I will give you rest" (Matthew 11:28).

Jesus promised to take our burdens and exchange them for His light load. "Take my yoke upon you and learn from me, for I am gentle and humble in heart, and you will find rest for your souls. For my yoke is easy and my burden is light" (vv. 29–30).

This promise is backed by His great strength. Whatever burdens we may carry, in Christ we find the strong shoulders of the Son of God, who promises to take our heavy burdens and exchange them for His light load.

Christ, who loves us with an everlasting love, understands our struggles, and He can be trusted to provide us with a rest we can never find on our own. His strength is enough for our weakness, making Him our "sanctuary for the heavy laden."

• • •

God calls the restless ones to find their rest in Him.

The Upside of Setbacks

Psalm 27

Wait for the LORD; be strong and take heart
and wait for the LORD. *Psalm 27:14*

American swimmer Dara Torres had a remarkable career, appearing in five different Olympics from 1984 to 2008. Late in her career, Torres broke the US record for the 50-meter freestyle—twenty-five years after she herself set that record. But it wasn't always medals and records. Torres also encountered obstacles in her athletic career: injuries, surgery, as well as being almost twice the age of most other competitors. She said, "I've wanted to win at everything, every day, since I was a kid. . . . I'm also aware that setbacks have an upside; they fuel new dreams."

"Setbacks have an upside" is a great life lesson. Torres's struggles motivated her to reach for new heights. They have a spiritual benefit too. As James said, "Consider it pure joy . . . whenever you face trials of many kinds, because you know that the testing of your faith produces perseverance" (James 1:2–3).

Adopting this perspective on the difficulties of life is not easy, but it is worthwhile. Trials provide opportunity to deepen our relationship with God. They also provide the opening to learn lessons that success cannot teach by developing in us the kind of patience that waits on God and trusts Him for the strength to endure.

The psalmist reminds us, "Wait for the LORD; be strong and take heart and wait for the LORD" (Psalm 27:14).

· · ·

The setbacks of life can teach us
to wait upon the Lord for His help and strength.

Ringing Reminders

Psalm 37:21–31

Though he may stumble, he will not fall,
for the LORD upholds him with his hand. *Psalm 37:24*

The clock tower at Westminster, which contains the bell known as Big Ben, is an iconic landmark in London. It is traditionally thought that the melody of the tower chimes was taken from the tune of "I Know That My Redeemer Liveth" from Handel's *Messiah*. Words were eventually added and put on display in the clock room:

Lord, through this hour be Thou our guide;

So by Thy power no foot shall slide.

These words allude to Psalm 37: "The LORD makes firm the steps of the one who delights him; though he may stumble, he will not fall, for the LORD upholds him with his hand" (vv. 23–24). Verse 31 adds, "The law of their God is in their hearts; their feet do not slip."

How extraordinary! The Creator of the universe not only upholds us and helps us but He also cares deeply about every moment we live. No wonder the apostle Peter was able to confidently invite us to "cast all your anxiety on him because he cares for you" (1 Peter 5:7). As the assurance of His care rings in our hearts, we find courage to face whatever comes our way.

• • •

No one is more secure than the one who is held in God's hand.

Wisdom and Grace

James 1:1–8

If any of you lacks wisdom, you should ask God. James 1:5

On April 4, 1968, American civil rights leader Dr. Martin Luther King Jr., was assassinated, leaving millions angry and disillusioned. In Indianapolis, a largely African American crowd had gathered to hear Robert F. Kennedy speak. Many had not yet heard of Dr. King's death, so Kennedy had to share the tragic news. He appealed for calm by acknowledging not only their pain but also his own abiding grief over the murder of his brother, President John F. Kennedy.

Kennedy then quoted a variation of an ancient poem by Aeschylus (526–456 BC):

> Even in our sleep, pain which cannot forget
> falls drop by drop upon the heart
> until, in our own despair, against our will,
> comes wisdom through the awful grace of God.

"Wisdom through the awful grace of God" is a remarkable statement. It means that God's grace fills us with awe and gives us the opportunity to grow in wisdom during life's most difficult moments.

James wrote, "If any of you lacks wisdom, you should ask God" (James 1:5). James says that this wisdom is grown in the soil of hardship (vv. 2–4), for there we not only learn from the wisdom of God but we also rest in the grace of God (2 Corinthians 12:9). In life's darkest times, we find what we need in Him.

• • •

The darkness of trials only makes God's grace shine brighter.

Serious Fear

Luke 2:8–20

Do not be afraid. I bring you good news
that will cause great joy for all the people. Luke 2:10

After weeks of preparation by the children's choir, the night had finally arrived for our annual Christmas musical. The costumed children began filing into the auditorium when suddenly we heard a ruckus at the back door. My wife and I turned to look and saw our own little Matt. Sobbing loudly and with a look of sheer terror on his face, he had a death grip on the door handle. He refused to enter the auditorium. After much negotiating, the director finally told him he didn't have to go on stage. Instead, Matt sat with us, and soon his fears began to subside.

Although we don't usually identify Christmas as a time of fear, there was plenty of it on the night of Christ's birth. Luke says, "An angel of the Lord appeared to them, and the glory of the Lord shone around them, and they were terrified" (Luke 2:9). The sight of the angelic messenger was more than the shepherds could process. But the angel reassured them: "Do not be afraid. I bring you good news that will cause great joy for all the people" (v. 10).

In a world full of fear, we need to remember that Jesus came to be the Prince of Peace (Isaiah 9:6). We desperately need His peace. As we look to Him, He will ease our fears and calm our hearts.

• • •

God incarnate is the end of fear. —F. B. Meyer

Also by Bill Crowder

• • •

Spread the Word
by Doing One Thing.

- Give a copy of this book as a gift.
- Share the QR code link via your social media.
- Write a review of this book on your blog, favorite bookseller's website, or at ODB.org/store.
- Recommend this book to your church, small group, or book club.

Connect with us. 🅕 ⓘ 🐦

Our Daily Bread Publishing
PO Box 3566, Grand Rapids, MI 49501, USA
Email: books@odb.org